China and Japan in the Global Setting

THE EDWIN O. REISCHAUER LECTURES, 1989

*Sponsored by the Dillon Fund under the auspices of
the John King Fairbank Center for East Asian Research*

China and Japan in the Global Setting

Akira Iriye

HARVARD UNIVERSITY PRESS
Cambridge, Massachusetts
London, England
1992

Library of Congress Cataloging-in-Publication Data

Iriye, Akira.
        China and Japan in the global setting / Akira Iriye.
            p.   cm.
        "The Edwin O. Reischauer lectures, 1989"—Half t.p.
        Includes bibliographical references and index.
        ISBN 0-674-11838-3
            1. Japan—Relations—China.   2. China—Relations—Japan.
        I. Title.   II. Title: Edwin O. Reischauer lectures.
        DS849.C6I78   1992
        303.48′251052—dc20   92-18965
                                              CIP

To the Memory of
EDWIN O. REISCHAUER

Preface

Like all Reischauer lecturers, I was asked to address a topic that embraces and connects the countries of East Asia. I chose to focus on the modern history of Chinese-Japanese relations. This may have been a reckless undertaking, since my work in the last twenty years or so has moved away from East Asian history per se, so my knowledge or understanding of this history may be somewhat dated.

I can attempt, however, to put Chinese-Japanese relations in a global context. My research and teaching for some time have been in international history, the history of modern international relations broadly defined, and I have found it useful to discuss the ways in which Chinese-Japanese relations have been affected by developments in the international community as a whole, and, at the same time, have contributed to defining it. It is my hope that this book will help clarify the nature of the interconnection between the bilateral relationship and global developments.

To give specificity to the topic I have divided the modern history of Chinese-Japanese relations into three periods: from the 1880s to the First World War; from the end of that war to the Second World War; and the post-1945 years. Each period is discussed in terms of three themes or dimensions: power, culture, and economics. Chinese-Japanese relations at the power level entail armaments, wars, strategies, security considerations, and the like and assume that each is a military power. Their economic-level relations involve trade, shipping, investment, emigration, and related activities, and each country is regarded as an econonic entity. At the cultural level the two countries interact or communicate by exchanging individuals, ideas, technology, and other "cultural productions"; thus we are talking of China and Japan as cultures. Of course some products of a culture may not be communicated at all, but that too would be part of the story. We must identify those ideas and artifacts that are readily transmitted across national boundaries and those that are less so, such as a nation's "core values," self-centered ideologies, or prejudices. The cultural dimension cannot be easily subsumed under the category of power or of economics, so it seems best to consider the three as overlapping but not necessarily interchangeable factors.

Although each of the three periods can—and will—be examined in terms of all three themes, it seems to me that during the first period power was decisive in determining the shape of Chinese-Japanese relations, just as the second and the third periods were notable because of the critical importance played by cultural and economic issues, respectively. I have named my three chapters accordingly.

I am grateful to the Council on East Asian Studies at Harvard University for having invited me to deliver the Reischauer lectures. It was my privilege to present them in November 1989. I dedicate this book to the memory of Professor Reischauer as a small token of my indebtedness to him as a scholar, teacher, and friend. In revising and expanding the lectures for publication, I have benefited from the comments received from many friends and colleagues, in particular Professors Chalmers Johnson and William Kirby. To all of them I would like to express my thanks. Ann Louise McLaughlin of Harvard University Press was my editor when I published my first book in 1965. I am most pleased and grateful that she once again agreed to help me and has edited this manuscript with her characteristic thoroughness and good sense.

Cambridge, Massachusetts   A. I.

Contents

I

Power

When discussing relations between two or more countries, it is customary to stress power, that is, the ways in which they respect, defend, or infringe upon each other's sovereignty and independence. These are power-level phenomena in that ultimately each nation must justify its existence by its ability to defend itself, and that entails military power, actual or potential, exercised unilaterally or in combination with the power of other countries. Power here does not mean armed force alone; it includes demography, natural resources, productivity, technology, and similar things that can be translated into military capabilities. Still, international relations in the power framework define nations fundamentally as military powers. They are seen as great or lesser powers depending on the size, extent, and effectiveness of their armed force. International relations, in short, are seen as inter-power relations.

Nations also interact economically through such activities as trade, shipping, investment, and migration. Here each country is definable as an economic unit, and international relations connote transactions among such economies. The fostering of commerce, industry, agriculture, and so on within the national boundary; the marketing of the products of such pursuits overseas; the search for foodstuffs and energy resources elsewhere—these constitute economic-level interactions among nations. Whereas the power-level relationship presupposes the potential existence of war as a possibility, economic interrelations do not necessarily imply international conflict, though that of course can also come about.

Traditionally these two aspects have been the main concern of historians of international relations. They have described in minute detail the geopolitical realities of power balances and their breakdowns, the formation and deformation of alliances, the development of military strategies, and the coming and ending of wars. They have also chronicled negotiations for treaties of commerce, international commercial rivalries, or cross-national loans and investment. Frequently the power and economic aspects are combined, for example, in studies of colonial empires which are both power-level and economic-level phenomena. These are most often the objects of study by students of international relations, and studies of Chinese-Japanese relations are no exception. Most studies of the bilateral relationship have dealt with war, diplomacy, trade, and related topics.

In addition to these two frameworks—power and economics—historians increasingly are becoming interested in the cultural aspect of international relations. Here a nation is defined as a culture, so international relations become intercultural relations. Culture, defined anthropologically, refers to a system of symbols or structures of meaning that provide some order for a given set of individuals. The nation is one large set of individuals; to view it as a culture means we must consider the images, meanings, and things they (and their progenitors) produce—their "cultural productions." Intercultural relations entail interactions among different cultures thus defined. Questions raised in this framework deal with the ways images, memories, ideas, life-styles, and artifacts are communicated across national boundaries, and how such activities affect, transform, or come into conflict with the cultural productions of other countries. Some visions and preoccupations may be shared across national boundaries; a sort of transnational or even global awareness may develop, as well as common behavior patterns in different parts of the world. It is obvious that at this level the nation is no longer the only, or even the most important, framework of analysis. Ideas, emotions, tastes, and fashions that cut across national boundaries may develop a life of their own, just as military balances of power or foreign trade and investment may. Ultimately, moreover, since culture cannot exist apart from individual men and women, the cultural framework is the most "human" of international relations. To borrow Joseph Nye's phrase, military force and economic activities may comprise "hard" power, whereas cultural pursuits and interactions may belong in the realm of "soft" power.[1] In any event, the cultural approach to international relations has served to broaden historical inquiry and added a rich variety of new questions to be addressed by historians.

Although three dimensions of international relations— power, economics, and culture—overlap and affect one another, they are by no means synonymous or interchangeable. Today's world may be characterized, first, by a balance of nuclear power that has, presumably, served to maintain what some have called "the long peace" since 1945. The United States is the reigning superpower, but until recently the Soviet Union played a role as the other nuclear giant, and the two, explicitly and implicitly, eschewed the use of nuclear force that would destroy the globe. Besides them, other nations maintain various types and degrees of armed power and occasionally impinge upon one another's sovereignty. Alliances and regional security arrangements are worked out so as to minimize instability.

The international order thus defined is quite different from a global economic system where goods, capital, resources, and technology are exchanged among nations and regions. Here the United States is not the hegemonic power that it is in the military sphere. Germany, Japan, and other nations of Europe and Asia, as well as the oil-rich countries of the Middle East, play key roles in shaping how people live. It is not so much military dispositions or the scale of armament that defines the world order in this context, as rates of exchange, the openness of domestic markets, or the level of technological expertise. Severe commercial disputes can occur even between military allies—as witness Japan and the United States.

Today's world may also be defined in terms of culture that range from the concern of people everywhere for elementary education to cross-national fashions in design, from shared aspirations for freedom and human rights to common concerns with the protection of the natural environment. The level of literacy, the quality of life, the degree of freedom—these and other "soft" phenomena, not its military power or economic prowess, are the indices of a country's greatness. To the extent that political developments in Poland, China, or South Africa arouse the interest of the rest of the world and generate support for certain segments of their populations, there develops a shared cultural universe throughout the world. Literary, artistic, or musical works that are enjoyed worldwide add to the definition of the international cultural order.

An intriguing question for the historian to ask would be in what ways these three definitions of the world relate to one another at a given moment in time. Does a certain world order defined in power terms facilitate its definitions in economic and cultural terms? If there is a significant gap between the power-defined world order and the economically defined world order, how would the gap be narrowed? Would the cultural world order play a role in the process?

The same types of questions can be asked of each country. One may ask what role it plays in the international system in the power, economic, and cultural spheres; which role it wishes to stress; and what happens if there are serious gaps between these roles. One can add intriguing questions such as: What happens if a country which defines its approach to the world primarily in power terms confronts another that gives priority to economic or cultural factors? What will their relationship tell about the wider world? Who in the domestic system is the determinant of such issues? Is there one structure of leadership that stresses one dimension of its foreign affairs and another that wishes to focus on something else? These are fascinating inquiries which should enrich our understanding of international relations and elucidate how domestic and international affairs are interconnected.

Students of Chinese and Japanese history have tended to distinguish between those who are interested in the foreign affairs of the two countries and those whose primary concern is with their internal affairs. But the modern destinies of both nations have been so intertwined that it is neither possible nor sensible to separate the two spheres. We need a perspective that can interpret what is happening inside China and Japan—and what is taking place between them. We must also go a step farther and relate these phenomena to developments in the rest of Asia and in the entire world; after all, China and Japan do not exist in isolation. It seems to me that the threefold scheme of power, economics, and culture helps in such an attempt, for these three categories deal with activities both within and between countries.

I propose to examine Chinese-Japanese relations from the late nineteenth century to the present. I will divide this century-long period into three: from the 1880s to the First

World War; from the end of that war to the beginning of another global conflagration; and the post–Second World War period. Each period will be examined in terms of the power, economic, and cultural dimensions of Chinese-Japanese relations, linking them to their respective domestic developments and to the overall international order. This is a formidable undertaking for a small book, but I think some interpretive cohesiveness may be achieved if I stress one predominant theme in each period. Power can serve as the overriding theme for the pre-1914 period, culture for the 1920s and the 1930s, and economics for the post-1945 years. We can discuss whether, to the extent that one theme (power, economics, or culture) was predominant in Chinese-Japanese relations at a given moment, that was also true of the internal affairs of the two countries, and of the overall international system. If the international system stressed one theme but Chinese-Japanese relations were characterized by the strong presence of another, how can we explain the difference? Were the domestically predominant themes also ones that defined Chinese-Japanese relations? If not, how can we account for this?

The first period, from the late nineteenth century to the First World War, corresponded to the last years of the Ch'ing dynasty and to the reign of the Meiji emperor. Although it is possible to pay equal attention to the power, economic, and cultural aspects of the two countries and their relationship at this time, I particularly stress the power theme, for it seems to have united the experiences of the two countries then. Chinese and Japanese elites shared a determination to transform their countries into militarily strong ones. They saw the mighty nations of the West primarily as military powers, with strong arms, a powerful class of military leaders, and overseas bases, colonies, and spheres of influence. Such perceptions made a decided impression on the elites—those who held political power and influence—in China and Japan, and they became convinced that their countries should develop similar features.

There was nothing inevitable about such thinking, for the leaders in the two countries had not always viewed themselves or the world in a framework defined in terms of military power. It would be wrong to say that China's traditional elites had been entirely unfamiliar with the idea of power defined in military terms, but in contrast to the West, Chinese political and bureaucratic/intellectual leaders had tended to see themselves as belonging to a society that was conceptualized more as a culture (or a civilization) than as a military power. This seems to have been the case as early as the Han period. Military force had at best been a necessary evil to maintain domestic order, not something in which the society would take particular pride or through which it would compare itself with others. Wars had been fought of course, but, in contrast to the West, where the multiple existence of nation-states after the sixteenth century almost always presupposed the possibility of war, in China most military conflicts took the form of protecting the Middle Kingdom against the nomads, barbarians of the steppes. Within the Great Wall, which separated the two kinds of societies, military force was of much less significance than culture as a symbol of authority and greatness.

It would be interesting to investigate when the Chinese began to view their country as a military power. By the 1870s, some at least were speaking of the need to build up armed force to cope with the changing world around China. This period corresponded to a particular phase in modern European history where five or six modern nation-states defined themselves as great powers and viewed each other as potential enemies. As Michael Howard has written, modern nations first defined themselves through an alienation from, a conflict with, or a triumph over other countries. Foreigners were "people with whom one went to war and almost always defeated." Paul Kennedy's recent book recounts how the European nations, later joined by the United States, were engaged in a constant drama of going up or down the scale of relative power, which was measured almost invariably in terms of a nation's ability to wage war successfully.[2]

It would be wrong to say that such developments in the Western state system were automatically transplanted into Asia. But the fact remains that China became steadily incorporated into the system, an incorporation that took the form not only of further Western penetration into that country but also China's military strengthening. Even so, the initial impetus in this direction seems to have come from the authorities' need to preserve domestic order. Historians generally agree that it was not so much the Opium War as the Taiping rebellion that brought about the military strengthening of the Ch'ing empire. Its purpose was to suppress a domestic uprising that presented a formidable threat to the internal system rather than to cope with an external crisis. It is important to recall that Li Hung-chang's Huai army, first organized by the scholar-gentry as a provincial force to combat the Taipings, later gained official recognition as the armed power of the country and went on to constitute the core of the fighting force against the Japanese army in 1894. The Huai army, like Tseng Kuo-fan's Hsiang army and several other provincial forces, was a national military force only in the sense that the Ch'ing dynasty gave it official endorsement; the recruitment and the training of its officers were done at the provincial level, and its units were commanded by men who were closely related to one another.

Nevertheless, Chinese leaders recognized armed force as the key to power—whether dynastic, national, or provincial. The Taiping experience revealed that the survival of the state ultimately depended on military power, and thus there steadily grew an awareness that the state's armed force was what kept the country together and, equally significant, strengthened its position vis-à-vis other countries. Sir Frederick Bruce, the British minister during the uprising, clearly saw the transformation that was taking place in China: the dawning awareness of the importance of military power and the will to develop one on the part of several high officials. Although the provincial nature of the new armed units remained, outwardly they had the appearance of modern armies being developed elsewhere. Li's Huai army, for instance, was equipped with rifles and cannons that were imported from Europe or produced at the Kiangnan arsenal. The arsenal contained a foreign-language school where Western books on military, business, and scientific affairs were translated. Most of the funds for the armed forces and arms factories came from customs revenue and *likin* (transit taxes) under Li's control, not from a national treasury. Li Hung-chang seems to have augmented or reduced the size of the army as he saw fit. In the early 1880s there were altogether 45,000 troops under his control, but in 1885 he dismissed over 10,000 of them to save money.[3]

The story was more or less the same regarding the establishment of a modern Chinese navy. In the 1860s the Foochow shipyard was constructed through the initiative of Tseng Kuo-fan, Li Hung-chang, and Tso Tsung-t'ang, and after 1875 naval ships were imported from Europe also.

These became the nucleus of the Peiyang navy, commanded by Ting Er-ch'ang, originally of the Huai army. In 1885 the navy *yamen* (office) was established, indicating awareness of the need to centralize naval policy and administration. In reality, however, Li continued to control matters in his capacity as governor-general of Chihli province. But after the mid-1880s, because of financial difficulties no foreign ships were purchased, and the Peiyang fleet had to depend on customs and likin receipts forwarded from various provinces, rather than counting on a centralized system of disbursement.

The fact remains that by the 1890s China had begun to build up modern military power. Although it was far from being a national armed force comparable to that of a European country, or even that in Japan, the stress on military power as an essential condition of national existence was clear. The thinking and behavior of leaders such as Tseng Kuo-fan and Li Hung-chang indicates that they were coming to view China's existence in the world in military terms and were willing to use force to demonstrate that the country would strengthen itself militarily in order to ensure its survival and preservation. Military power was not as centralized as in some other nations, but the leaders were coming to accept the idea of national defense. In a famous memorial to the throne after the opening of hostilities against Japan in 1894, Li compared the relative strengths and weaknesses of the two countries' navies. The language he used was virtually interchangeable with that of any military strategist in the West. He contrasted the number, the size, and the speed of the existing Chinese and Japanese ships, admitted that in a sea battle with Japan, China might lose because of the latter's superiority in new cruisers, but expressed optimism that the Japanese would be so overawed by

China's iron-clads in and near Pohai Bay that they would not dare commence an attack.[4] Li proved too optimistic, but the basic vocabulary he resorted to in his analysis was that of military power. It has sometimes been said that the Chinese elite like him who undertook the military strengthening of their country were misguided because they put their emphasis on armed force rather than on other aspects of modern nationhood such as industrialization or political reform. But it could just as plausibly be argued that the emphasis on military power was precisely what characterized the modern states of Europe and that, coming from a nonmilitary tradition, it was no mean achievement for the Chinese to accept the fact that, if their country were to gain respect abroad and to protect itself, they would first have to strengthen the armed forces. They would even have to be willing to go to war, for war was considered then the ultimate test of a nation's power.

China would lose that test in the war against Japan. The Meiji leaders, even more than their Chinese counterparts, had focused their efforts on military strengthening. As in China, the attempt was often frustrated by the existence of provincial centers of power which had defined the feudal system and did not disappear even after the Meiji Restoration. Unlike the Chinese scholar gentry who organized the new armed forces after the 1860s, however, the Meiji leaders came from the warrior (samurai) background, knew what was entailed in such efforts, and, above all, recognized the need for centralization of military power if the new government were to survive against both internal dissent and external threat. Starting with the abolition of the *han* (feudal domains) in 1871, intensive attempts were made to create centralized armed forces. It is interesting to note that the core of the new Japanese army consisted of some 6,000 men from what had been Satsuma, Chōshū, and Tosa han, those that had played major roles in bringing down the Tokugawa regime. This situation was not very different from the emergence of provincial armies in China during the 1860s and the 1870s. Soon, however, the two countries' armies began to differ, as the Meiji leaders launched a systematic campaign to establish a strong central army. This task may have been the more easily defined in Japan, for its officials shared a sense of external threat facing the country. Already in December 1871 Yamagata Aritomo and others were arguing that Japan needed to consider Russia its hypothetical enemy and strengthen its armed force against it. Japanese military power was obviously inferior, and therefore the nation must do all it could to catch up.

In the meantime, a Japanese navy had come into existence. The Meiji government, as a result of its victory in the brief civil war, took over the vessels belonging to the Tokugawa regime and to other han loyal to it, and plans were made to create a modern navy, again with Russia considered the most likely enemy. The fact that both army and navy leaders were speaking of an external threat to the nation's survival means that in the 1870s the Japanese already were accepting the language of modern military affairs, at the same time the Chinese were beginning to do so.

These parallel developments produced two modernized military forces in Asia. Initially most foreign observers were more impressed with Chinese than with Japanese achievements. It is interesting to recall that as of 1894 Chinese military power was, at least quantitatively, superior to Japanese. Prior to the outbreak of war, the Japanese army had been built up to a strength of about 60,000 men, while the navy had been increased to twenty-eight ships. In contrast,

China had about 350,000 regular troops, including such traditional units as the Green Banners. The Chinese navy, with the Peiyang fleet at its core, consisted of seventy-one warships. Some of these ships and about 1,500 of the troops were sent to Korea at the request of the court in Seoul in July 1894, establishing China's military presence on the peninsula. Japan responded in kind, a step considered necessary, in the words of Foreign Minister Mutsu Munemitsu, "to maintain a power balance" between the two forces. Soon, however, the dispatching of Japanese troops went beyond such an objective, indicating that Tokyo's leaders had decided to seize the opportunity to rid Korea of Chinese power and influence.[5] China's numerical advantages in army and naval strength were overcome by Japan's swift and decisive action, including rapid mobilization and the establishment of the General Headquarters. Although the first Chinese-Japanese war, like all wars, had diplomatic, economic, and domestic political implications, it was in our context as classical a case of the clash of two powers as any: two neighboring countries used military force to test each other at the expense of a weaker third country. The result, as had happened so often in Europe, was the further weakening and eventual disappearance of the victim and the relative rise in power of the victor.

Having established military superiority over China, the Japanese went on to reinforce that power through colonial acquisitions. This too was in accordance with the prevailing notions about power, for by the 1890s military power had come to include not only arms and armed forces but also overseas bases, colonies, and spheres of influence. It was a geopolitical definition of power, and as such it was interchangeable with imperialism. For the Meiji leaders few Western ideas could have been easier to comprehend and incorporate than this. By then they had become accustomed to viewing the European nations as self-aggrandizing colonialists bent upon extending their sway over the rest of the world. It took little hesitation for the Japanese leaders, therefore, to decide on China's cession of the Liaotung Peninsula, Taiwan, and the Pescadores as conditions for peace. All these territories had strategic significance: Liaotung for safeguarding Japan's new position in Korea, and Taiwan and its vicinity for providing bases for the navy. Above all, these possessions would signal Japan's status as a new major power, and such a status would in turn ensure national independence and prestige in the age of colonial powers.

When the design was temporarily frustrated as a result of the Russian-French-German intervention, purely military considerations again led to Japan's acceptance of the humiliating intercession. Not because Tokyo's leaders had any second thoughts about the morality or economic wisdom of acquiring and administering colonies taken from China, but because they agreed they had no chance of going to war against the combined forces of those nations, they decided to beat a temporary retreat. As it happened, the Japanese army had trouble even in bringing Taiwan under control, as the island's inhabitants put up fierce resistance, so that it would have been totally out of the question to try to hold on to the southern Manchurian territory. It was only after the pacification of Taiwan that Japan turned next to Korea, to establish its suzereinty there, and that after that was partially accomplished it went on to fight a war against Russia to regain what it had given up in southern Manchuria.

By the turn of the century Japan's military superiority over China had been well established; henceforth their relationship would be one of a rising military power further strengthening itself at the expense of its weaker neighbor.

The Russo-Japanese war was a classic example of this pattern. The two powers fought against one another on Chinese soil to determine how to divide a portion of China (Manchuria) into spheres of influence. As a result of the war Japan entrenched itself in Liaotung Peninsula and gained possession of the Changchun-Talien (Dairen) portion of the Russian-controlled Chinese Eastern Railway. In order to protect the newly acquired rights, a Kwantung army was created, the symbol of Japan's continental imperialism.

The Chinese were not merely passive victims of Japanese imperialism. As before, the reforms the Ch'ing court undertook in the wake of the Chinese-Japanese war stressed military power. In fact it was during the war that rudiments of a new army, to replace the by then decrepit Huai army, were established. Consisting of 7,400 men, it constituted the core of the Peiyang army, under the command first of Jung Lu and then of Yüan Shih-k'ai. Employing German advisers and using modern weapons, the Peiyang army was instrumental in suppressing the Boxers. The Ch'ing court was so impressed with Yüan's successes in Shantung Province that it sought to organize a similar army in each province, to be under the overall supervision of a ministry of war.[6] Some of the new provincial armies were commanded by Chinese officers who had been sent to Japan for training at the War College. Ironically many of these officers, upon returning home, visualized themselves as provincial leaders aiming at local autonomy rather than as part of a unified national force. In addition, anti-Ch'ing revolutionaries began organizing their own armed units and infiltrating the provincial armies as well. As a result, when the European war erupted in 1914, China was militarily divided and no centralized army had been established.

Comparing China and Japan in the decades preceding the

First World War, we may conclude that in the military sphere the former failed to develop as a modern state, whereas the latter succeeded. But this success was also at the expense of China's failure, so the two phenomena were closely linked. The Meiji Japanese learned from China's disastrous wars with the European nations, made war on China in turn, and established their country as a colonial power by snatching territory away from China. There was a Japanese contribution to the making of modern Chinese military power through the training of Chinese officers in Japan, but this had the effect of preparing them as revolutionaries against the Manchu dynasty and, in some instances, as provincial leaders who would become local warlords. It was symbolic that in 1915 Yüan Shih-k'ai, one Chinese leader who had done much to modernize the country's military force, was powerless to resist Japanese demands—the so-called twenty-one demands—for more territorial concessions. The episode ultimately led to his disgrace and death, causing a further division of China into fragments under the control of local warlords, while Japan went on to emerge from the World War as one of the three major military powers of the world.

In accounting for the divergent paths trodden by China and Japan, one should not lose sight of the larger picture, the international context as it had been developed by the Western powers. As noted earlier, the world order was dominated by a small number of sovereign nations, each a military power. As such it could easily accommodate Japan as the newest member of the community of nations because it had the essential prerequisites for membership: armaments, successful military campaigns, and colonies. Japan would play the game of power politics and in the process not only extend its control over weaker countries but also transgress upon other powers' interests and prerogatives—but that was common practice. China, on the other hand, did not quite fit into the system. Although some countries, notably the United States, spoke of upholding its territorial and administrative integrity, there was something incongruous in this age of the great powers to have a nation whose sovereignty had to be ensured through international goodwill. It would not, and did not, work, and China remained weak, a mere shadow of its former self—one whose grandeur, however, had not been built on military strength.

There was another way in which Japan's emergence as a military power came at the expense of China. The reparations payment of 200 million tael, about 360 million yen, that China paid Japan in 1895 not only defrayed Japan's costs of the war—which were estimated to have amounted to 247 million yen—but also provided funds for the construction of the Yawata Iron Works, the first modern factory built during the Meiji era. This reflects the fact that, potentially at least, China was richer than Japan, but that Japan made more effective use of its limited resources by focusing on military strengthening.

This leads to the second level of comparison between China and Japan, their economic resources and performance. As of 1800 China was probably the richest country in the world. It was unsurpassed in population, output (including manufacturing, where China accounted for one-third of the world's total production), and natural resources. The picture had changed completely a century later, when the world's still most populous country could account for only 6 percent of the world's total manufacturing output. This had resulted from the West's industrialization and rapidly expanding trade, which went hand in hand. But if China had become relatively impoverished, Japan had always been poor. Although its population increased by 50 percent during the Meiji era, arable land did not, and acreage for rice production remained more or less fixed, necessitating the import of this and other staples. Japan was so lacking in minerals that domestic iron accounted for less than 10 percent of what was used for cannons during the Chinese-Japanese war.[7] The country was self-sufficient only in coal, but that condition ended with the war, after which increasing quantities had to be brought in from Korea, Manchuria, and Sakhalin, one reason for the interest in controlling these areas. As for industrialization, at the turn of the century fewer than one million Japanese—about 2 percent of the population—worked in factories employing more than five persons. This seems to have been about the same proportion of the population in China then engaged in manufacturing. The only area where Japan did better at that time probably was railway construction. Since the 1870s there had been a systematic national effort to build railroads; even so, prior to the Chinese-Japanese war less than one thousand kilometers had been laid, not much more than the Chinese had built or at least developed plans for. (In those days in the West railroads were increasingly becoming incorporated into military strategies, and the Japanese recognized the connection far sooner than the Chinese. The fact that the latter failed for a long time to develop a national network of railroads was to prove a major handicap standing in the way of its military unification.)

Another interesting set of comparisons is foreign trade. In 1894 Japan exported something like 113 million yen worth of goods and imported 117 million yen. The 4-million-yen deficit was a harbinger of things to come. Between 1894 and 1914 there was a chronic trade deficit, as Japan imported more and more goods from both Asia and the West, which its growing export could not match. The need for imports may be explained by Japan's increasing population as well as the requirements of industrialization. As it launched modest industrialization programs, Japan had to import raw materials and machinery and pay for them by exporting the products of its nascent industry, initially limited to cotton spinning and weaving. Few Japanese knew how to create industrial machinery, so engineers from Germany, Britain, and elsewhere had to be brought in as instructors. Ship-building, an essential arm of foreign trade, was still in its early stages, and during the Meiji era Japanese shipyards lacked the skills and machinery to produce large-sized ships of more than 2,000 tons. These had to be purchased from abroad, another factor contributing to balance-of-trade deficits.

In contrast, China was not a major trading nation, since it produced most of the goods its people consumed. The country as a whole had developed as a huge market, with internal trade suppplying most of the necessities of people throughout the empire. The situation did not change significantly, even after the collapse of the dynasty in 1911. It is estimated, for instance, that as of 1918 an average Chinese person exported 1.6 gold dollar's worth of goods and imported 1.9 gold dollars, whereas for the average Japanese the figures were 14.3 and 16.0 gold dollars respectively.[8] In other words, Japan's dependence on foreign trade may be said to have been eight or nine times as great as that of China's. It is also true, however, that, like Japan, China had perennial trade deficits. This was basically because it had to import large quantities of goods such as kerosene and cotton yarn from abroad, which had to be paid for by exporting food and raw materials such as tea and silk. What is interesting at the same time is the flow of gold—and in China's case silver—as these metals were taken as indicators of balance of payments. During the first ten years of the twentieth century more gold tended to flow out of Japan than came in, showing that the country's trade deficits were not made up for by other kinds of revenue from abroad. Because at that time gold was considered the key measure of a country's financial standing, Japan remained quite low on this scale, lower than China, where larger quantities of both gold and silver tended to flow in than go out, as a result of remittances from overseas Chinese and investments and loans by foreigners. Of course Japan too borrowed money from abroad, especially after the Russian war, but foreign investment remained very limited. China seemed a more attractive market for European and American capitalists than Japan.

Despite this rather dismal picture, Japan did launch its industrialization following the war with China. Nevertheless, prior to the World War it ranked far below most Western countries in terms of capital accumulation, manufacturing output, and per-capita income. For instance, Japan's national income in 1914 was estimated to have been about 2,443 million yen, which comes to less than 50 yen per person, or about 25 dollars. This may have been slightly higher than comparable figures for China, but it was definitely below the per-capita incomes of the advanced countries of the West. Even on the eve of the World War, Japan was essentially an agricultural country, with more than three-quarters of its population engaged in farming.

It was not until the European war that Japan accelerated the tempo of industrialization—but so did China. Both countries took advantage of Europe's temporary absence from Asia and began producing goods hitherto supplied by European manufacturers. In Japan the industrial population nearly doubled between 1914 and 1919, although more than 80 percent of the people still lived in rural areas. The number of factories employing more than five workers rose from 31,000 in 1914 to 43,000 in 1919. Even more impressive was the phenomenal growth in Japan's foreign trade. During the war, for the first time since the end of the nineteenth century the country was able to record significant trade surpluses. Japanese exports grew from 591 million yen in 1914 to nearly 2 billion four years later, a threefold increase, whereas imports grew less rapidly. As a result, in 1918 there was a trade surplus of nearly 300 million yen. This helped create balance-of-payments surpluses for the first time since the opening of the country. There was also a large outflow of funds from Japan in the form of overseas loans and investments, as well as repayment of money borrowed earlier. In 1918, for example, funds totaling 615 million yen, three times the amount in 1914, were shipped abroad, but this was more than offset by the inflow of 685 million yen, representing trade surpluses, shipping charges, and returns on loans and investments overseas. It would be correct to say that it took the European war to industrialize Japan.

The same was more or less true of China, for it too began developing "import-substituting" industries to make up for the disappearance of European goods. Cotton textiles, cigarettes, matches, and other mass-produced commodities now replaced, substantially if not totally, foreign imports. As in Japan, there was a migration of people from rural to urban areas, and a class of industrial capitalists emerged. Unlike Japan, China did not enjoy trade surpluses during the war, but its trade deficits declined visibly. Whereas before the European war there had been annual deficits of more than 100 million tael, in 1915 the figure fell to 35 million, and in 1919 to 16 million. This undoubtedly was the result of Chinese industrialization, as reflected in the fact that the import of cotton yarn steadily declined during these years. In 1918 there were thirty-four cotton textile factories in China, equipped with close to one million spindles, enough to make up for the loss of European imports.

Despite such parallel developments, by the end of the First World War, Japan had come to surpass China in terms of certain economic indicators. It was now a net exporter of goods and capital, and it was industrializing in areas such as cotton weaving, chemicals, and machine goods where China was still underdeveloped. Of course Japan was not wealthy by Western standards. In 1919 its per-capita income had reached 100 yen, about 50 dollars, but this was still below the incomes even of the war-devastated nations of Europe, not to mention the United States whose per-capita income was at least ten times that of Japan's. Still, comparing China and Japan, the conclusion is inescapable that the latter had begun to outstrip the former in economic performance. To the extent that both Chinese and Japanese leaders in this period had developed visions of "rich country, strong army" (a term not unknown in premodern China, but one that was rediscovered and adopted as a national slogan by both China and Japan in the last decades of the nineteenth century), Japan's was a more successful story.

An interesting question in this context would be the extent to which Japan's success was achieved at the expense of China. The question can be examined at a number of levels. For one thing, it cannot be denied that much of Japan's economic gain had come about because China offered it reparations, territory rich in resources, and easily accessible markets for trade and investment. Without the reparations of 1895, without the cession of Taiwan and the lease of the Liaotung Peninsula, and without the unequal treaties Japan forced upon China which kept import duties low and protected foreign merchants and industrialists from Chinese jurisdiction, Japanese industrialization would have been much slower than it actually was. Japanese exports to China doubled after the war of 1894–95, tripled after the Russo-Japanese war, and quadrupled during the European war. And Japan's share in Chinese imports increased from less than 3 percent before the Chinese-Japanese war to more than 10 percent after the Russo-Japanese war and to around 30 percent during the World War. There were parallel increases in China's share in Japanese imports, but Japan continued to enjoy substantial surpluses in the bilateral trade. Because, as noted earlier, Japan suffered from chronic trade deficits until 1914, especially with regard to the Western nations, the favorable balance of trade vis-à-vis China was one bright spot in the picture. Conversely, for China this meant that a significant portion—sometimes as much as 40 percent—of its overall trade deficit was accounted for by the Japanese trade. So in some sense China unwittingly assisted Japan's economic modernization.[9]

Another way of putting the equation might be to say that China was initially and always potentially a far richer country than Japan, but that its military weakness left it at the mercy of its stronger neighbor. Was military power the key factor? It is fashionable today to argue that economic modernization is closely connected with, in fact assisted by, military modernization.[10] Thus it could be observed that the needs of war against China in the 1890s stimulated the growth of iron, ship-building, and other industries in Japan. Military strengthening enabled Japan to defeat China and collect huge reparations, the basis for initial Japanese industrialization. In addition, Japan's enhanced status as a military power won the grudging respect of the Western powers and persuaded them to abandon their unequal treaties, including restrictions on tariff autonomy. Once Japan gained the right to determine import duties without consulting other countries, it became much easier to encourage domestic production by barring imports. For all these reasons, the priority given to military strengthening, which was often at the expense of China, may have been the only alternative if Japan were to undertake economic transformation.

Such assertions need to be put in perspective by a counterfactual proposition: Would Japan not have made even greater economic gains if it had not spent so much on arms and wars? Would the economies both of China and of Japan not have been beneficiaries of peace rather than of war? The share of military expenditures in Japan's annual budgets ranged roughly between 30 and 50 percent during 1890–1919, even without counting the supplementary appropriations for the wars of 1894–95 and 1904–05. Because government outlays amounted to 30–40 percent of the national income—double incidentally of comparable figures among Western nations—this meant that 10 and sometimes as much as 20 percent of the national income went into military spending. Added to this were expenses required to maintain a colonial empire, which was reflected in the fact that after 1895 the administrative expense category in the governmental budget doubled, tripled, and quadrupled within a few years. Obviously the Japanese people had to put up with such expenditures, which had to be financed through various taxes as well as government monopolies and foreign loans. Compared with the Western countries, much less proportionally was being spent on social programs, and much less remained in private hands to pursue economic and cultural activities. The country might have been better off if less had been spent on war and empire, and certainly China would have been better off if Japan had not decided to devote a larger portion of its resources than any other nation to war and empire.

It is difficult to speculate whether the increasingly close economic ties between China and Japan would have grown even closer if Japanese military and strategic considerations had been less prominent, and whether such ties would have been to the benefit of China. Without Japan's increasingly assertive military presence in Manchuria or its blatantly aggressive behavior as exemplified by the twenty-one demands episode, the Chinese might have been more inclined to accept Japanese goods or import Japanese technology rather than trying to boycott them as they did in 1908, 1915, and 1919. If military priorities had not been so decisive in Japanese approaches to China, the law of comparative advantages might have functioned in such a way as to develop the two economies' complementarity.[11] On the other hand, such a situation might have perpetuated the situation of China's being always a step behind Japan in economic development. It is worth raising such speculative questions, for there was nothing inevitable about Japan's decision to give top priority to military and strategic considerations.

The fact remains that in Japan's approach to China and to international affairs in general during the Meiji era, power took precedence over economics. The emphasis on power becomes even more evident when we examine the cultural aspect, the third dimension of Chinese-Japanese relations at that time. This aspect was by no means insignificant. There were substantial cultural interactions—or the building of networks of communication, as I would characterize the cultural dimension of international relations—between the two countries. But this was not the determinant factor in the overall bilateral relationship in the years before the end of the First World War. There was a wide disparity between the military and cultural dimensions of Chinese-Japanese relations just as there was a gap between their power and economic aspects.

The extent of the cultural connection between Chinese and Japanese may first be seen in the growing mutual awareness and knowledge between the two peoples. This is not the usual view. Scholars who have examined Chinese and Japanese mutual perceptions have suggested misunderstanding, or indifference, or condescension, or arrogance—anything but communication. The Chinese are usually depicted as having clung to traditional images and looked down on Japan as a country of imitative dwarfs. They had not bothered to learn anything about Japan until it was too late. The Japanese in the Meiji era, for their part, avidly Westernized themselves until they no longer considered their country Asian, a member of the Chinese sphere of civilization. Fukuzawa Yukichi was only reiterating fairly widespread notions when, in the 1890s, he spoke of Japan's "leaving" Asia and joining the ranks of the advanced Western nations. The implication was that Japan would now refuse to be associated, let alone identified, with China. Such mutual arrogance and condescension was conducive to misunderstanding, a reflection of the two countries' antagonistic power relationship. So it has often been said.

But that is a distorted interpretation. It could be argued just as plausibly that the Chinese and the Japanese became more conscious of one another during the second half of the nineteenth century than ever before. They certainly obtained more information about one another through European and American intermediaries as well as through direct observation. The Japanese had been familiar with Chinese history for centuries, and they continued to read the Chinese classics. Now some Chinese officials and intellectuals began showing an interest in Japanese history, politics, and even culture and published a number of books about the country. One theme in these books was Japan's modernization. As Ch'en Chia-lin, who visited Japan as a member of the diplomatic mission of 1884, noted, the country had established new schools, opened mines, built railways, organized banks, and undertaken many other projects for national transformation.[12] The theme of rapid change in Japan had become standard by the 1890s, and it is not surprising that after the Chinese-Japanese war it was stressed even more, providing an impetus for those reformers who looked to Japan for inspiration. For a segment of the Chinese population, therefore, one would have to conclude that there was a willingness to be open-minded about the neighboring country and even to learn from it.

That also fitted into the perception of some Japanese who, unlike Fukuzawa, were interested in transmitting the blessings of modern civilization to China. Here we have to raise a number of questions. Although it must has been very easy for the Japanese to view China as less developed or modernized than Japan and thus in need of a civilizing mission by Japanese, did this indicate anything other than a superficial knowledge of China? It was reported that there was a serious shortage of Japanese with adequate knowledge of the Chinese language during the war of 1894–95.[13] The study of Chinese, apart from the classics, was not as prestigious as that of European languages; even after the war the language was taught only in schools and colleges specializing in military or commercial affairs. Balanced against this, however, is the fact that while the Chinese language may not have been widely taught, Chinese characters undoubtedly were. Meiji reforms did not entail any significant change in the Japanese writing system, which was rooted in the classical Chinese tradition, and schoolchildren continued to study the classics and memorize thousands of Chinese characters. And there were far more pupils studying them at the end than at the beginning of the Meiji era, roughly a sixfold increase from one to six million attending primary school. By 1919 there were, in addition to over seven million primary school students, one out of every seven Japanese, over two million were attending various types of secondary and higher institutions of learning. Numerically at least more Japanese than ever before were becoming familiar with aspects of Chinese civilization. The persistent influence of the Chinese classics can be detected in the letters exchanged among Japan's leaders which were littered with references to the classics. At the Shimonoseki peace conference of 1895 Foreign Minister Mutsu Munemitsu was able to read and comprehend what the Chinese delegate Li Hung-chang wrote in Chinese. No wonder that Li proclaimed that the two countries shared a common language. This was an exaggeration, for the episode revealed not so much a cultural sharing as Japan's cultural dependence on China even while its military might was proving superior. Mutsu's example, which can be multiplied, suggests that no matter how much one was influenced by Western civilization, Chinese learning was still considered a prerequisite for Japanese leaders. It was not enough in Meiji Japan merely to be steeped in English or French literature in order to be viewed a civilized person; one had to demonstrate a familiarity with the Chinese classics as well. Writers like Futabatei Shimei, Tsubouchi Shōyō, and Nagai Kafū come to mind. Their translations from European originals were rendered into literary Japanese, which contained complicated Chinese characters and sentence structures. Readers of literary works must have understood these characters. Similarly, newspapers catering to mass readership were written in the literary style (*bungotai*), which made extensive use of Chinese characters.

Knowledge of, or admiration for, the classics did not mean that the Japanese had a good understanding of contemporary China. But in the context of the time, when foreign observers overwhelmingly were depicting negative images of the faltering, corrupt, and backward society and culture of China, one could point to Japanese writers, travelers, and *shishi* (adventurers) who sought to understand the neighboring country and often described it lovingly. Many more became familiar with China as a result of direct experience as soldiers or colonists. Some 200,000 Japanese troops were in Manchuria at the end of the war in 1895, a measure of Japan's physical presence on the continent. Although they were soon repatriated, Japanese soldiers, colonial officials, railway workers, and others would return following the Russo-Japanese war. While Manchuria was not colonized the way Taiwan was, the number of Japanese residents engaged in retailing, farming, teaching, and other activities in the Liaotung Peninsula amounted to several thousands. In China proper about seven hundred Japanese were in the Peking-Tientsin area after the Russo-Japanese war, five hundred of whom as teachers in Chinese schools.[14] There were Japanese lawyers, journalists, students, and merchants in Shanghai, Nanking, and other cities, as well as shishi in the hinterland. Adding the increasing numbers of travelers to China, it may be estimated that at the end of the Ch'ing dynasty about ten thousand Japanese lived in various parts of China. This tiny fraction of the total Japanese population of fifty million was nevertheless the largest foreign contingent in China.

What impact did their experiences have on Japanese images of China? It is hard to generalize, for the writings by Japanese who were in China for different lengths of time ranged from arrogant, ethnocentric tracts to sympathetic portrayals. To take literary figures as examples, Kunikida Doppo, who accompanied the Japanese army into Manchuria in 1895, spread an unflattering image of Chinese as totally devoid of national consciousness. But a few years later Nagai Kafū found Shanghai a truly cosmopolitan city, unlike anything he had seen in Japan. During the Russo-Japanese war Yosano Akiko published loving depictions of Chinese peasants, while most writings focused on the corruption and backwardness of Ch'ing officials.[15] In the 1880s and the 1890s activists like Arao Sei and Taruo Tōkichi began formulating visions of the two countries cooperating to save East Asian civilization; those like Miyazaki Torazō threw in their lot with China's revolutionaries and depicted them as would-be patriots.[16]

It is impossible to determine how these various representations of China defined Japanese attitudes toward that country during the Meiji era, but it cannot be denied that many more Japanese than ever before developed an awareness of China and Chinese-Japanese relations. To the extent that cultural relations entail networking, here was a clear instance of the creation of numerous and interlocking networks of information which developed often distorted and contradictory images of China in Japanese minds but which nevertheless were not the exact parallels of either the military or the economic aspect of the bilateral relationship.

There was a Chinese counterpart to this cultural aware-

ness. China's contact with Japan at this time, like that with
other countries, was mainly through the presence of Japanese and other foreigners in the treaty ports, but in this
connection foreign teachers seem to have played a particularly significant role. One must remember that even as late
as 1911 only about 1,600,000 pupils were attending primary
school in China, a mere 2.5 percent of school-age children.[17]
But even though the number was small, the schools they
attended, many of them founded after the Boxer uprising,
symbolized China's serious attempt at cultural change. It is
difficult to separate out Japan's role in this transformation.
At least it may be noted that late-Ch'ing reformers turned
to Japan as well as to Europe and America for guidance,
and that Chinese children learned mathematics, science, and
other subjects from Japanese as well as from Western teachers. It is estimated that by the first decade of the century
some one hundred middle-school textbooks had been translated from Japanese into Chinese.[18] If we add Chinese translations of Japanese translations of Western books, we can
easily imagine the emergence of a new phenomenon in
Chinese-Japanese cultural relations in which Japan contributed to Chinese education virtually for the first time.

Chinese-Japanese contact also took place in Japan, which
attracted an increasing number of Chinese visitors, merchants, and students. Already in 1896 the first group of
thirteen Chinese students arrived in Tokyo, sent by their
government. They were followed by many other officially
and privately funded students, so that by 1905 there were
over 8,000 of them in Yokohama, Tokyo, and other cities.
Many were reformers or radicals, committed to the restructuring or overthrow of the dynasty, and a substantial number returned to China after the revolution of 1911. The size
of the Chinese student body in Japan would never again

reach this peak, for more and more of them would go to the United States or to Europe rather than to Japan. Even so, if we add up all the Chinese students abroad during the 1890s through 1919, we will probably find that more of them had been to Japan than to any other country. And more students were being sent abroad from China than from any other nation, so that this aspect of Chinese-Japanese relations constitutes a key element of the story.[19] It is difficult to ascertain precisely what the students in Japan learned. Sanetō Keishū, the leading authority on the subject, admitted in 1940 that Chinese students in Japan tended to consider the host country devoid of any culture worth emulating and had gone to Japan primarily to absorb Western learning more cheaply than by going to the West.[20] This may well have been true, but that does not diminish the importance of the cultural contact. In fact the Japanese during the Meiji era often stressed their role as a country successfully Westernizing itself and thus serving as an intermediary between China and the West. Most of the hundreds of Japanese books translated into Chinese were encyclopedias, legal treatises, technical works on agriculture, and the like, which Japanese authors had written on the basis of Western originals. Many Western terms and concepts were rendered into their Japanese equivalents through the use of Chinese characters, so that the Chinese could simply borrow Japanese translations instead of having to come up with their own version of terms like "sovereignty," "liberalism," "Renaissance," and "anarchy." If, therfore, cultural change was a significant phenomenon of Chinese history at that time, it would be difficult to ignore the Japanese connection.

All of this perhaps could be put in the framework of "cultural imperialism," a term that has been applied where a country establishes a major cultural presence in another country, whether it is a result of a conscious design or more a case of informal influences. American cultural influence, because it has been the most obvious, has been called "Coca-colonization," implying a cultural annexation of other countries through the ideas, goods, and tastes emanating from the United States. Was Japanese cultural influence in China a similar phenomenon? There is no doubt that there was substantial Japanese imput into the way in which the Chinese came to perceive themselves and the world at this time and to undertake their own transformation. Whether or not this was a case of Japan's controlling or "hegemonizing" over Chinese culture would be a more complicated proposition if only because the Japanese had never shaken off their cultural dependence on China, particularly in their literature and writing systems. Even if they had tried to do so, the Chinese would have repulsed such an attempt, convinced as they were that Japan's usefulness as a transmitter of Western civilization did not mean they had to come under the influence of other aspects of Japanese culture. In this connection, it may be noted that, in contrast to Westerners, the Japanese did not attempt to convert the Chinese to their religion, Shintoism, or Buddhism for that matter, although there were a few Japanese Buddhist missionaries here and there in parts of China. For most Chinese such missionary activities made little sense; after all, China had given Japan its Buddhist religion.

Instead of putting into the category of cultural imperialism everything from the opening of Japanese bookstores in Peking to the Ch'ing court's adoption of the Meiji constitution as a model, it would be better to say that cultural relations had their own momentum, and that not all of them were associated with Japan's military domination over China or with its economic activities. There was a significant gap between the cultural and military aspects of the bilateral relationship. The two countries' rather one-sided military relationship, characterized by Japanese power and control over China, was not exactly replicated in the cultural sphere. Another way of putting this would be to say that the two countries' close cultural contact did little to alter the basic pattern of Japan's military dominance. Add to this the primacy of military over economic affairs at that time that I have suggested, and we may conclude that the preeminent theme of Chinese-Japanese relations between the 1880s and the end of the First World War was power, in particular military force and influence. Economic and cultural affairs developed with their own momentum, but they did not affect the overall definition of the bilateral relationship in power terms.

Why should this have been the case? Why, if the foregoing summation makes sense, should military affairs and power calculations have been the ultimate determinant of Chinese-Japanese relations at that time? One factor was the emergence of the military in positions of power and influence in both China and Japan. The transformation of China's traditional elites, the scholar-gentry, into military leaders and warlords was a graphic illustration of this, as was the privileged status accorded Japan's armed forces in the budgetary and decisionmaking processes. In Japan's case the picture was initially less complicated than in China inasmuch as the Meiji transformation essentially perpetuated the status of former samurai as leaders. But the military's authority came to be challenged by party politicians, civilian bureaucrats, businessmen, and intellectuals. The story of Taishō democracy, to be discussed in Chapter II, is in essence that of a revolt against the military's privileged position. During most of the period prior to the 1920s, however, it would be hard to underestimate the fact that the nation's resources were focused primarily on military strengthening and that this both involved and reflected the power and influence of military leaders.

The primacy of the military factor in Chinese-Japanese relations at that time should also be understood in the context of the overall international system then, which too gave priority to military power. Pre-1914 international affairs were dominated by the European powers, which had become powers by virtue of having amassed armaments and colonies. To be sure they were also engaged in commercial transactions with one another, but their interrelations were characterized increasingly by military considerations. The liberal British view, popular in the earlier decades, that economics determined relations among nations was giving way to an emphasis on armaments and alliances. The European nations also interacted with one another culturally. Europeans from different countries went to each other's schools, museums, and opera houses to acquire a cosmopolitan outlook. But such ties were becoming less crucial than balance-of-power calculations. Despite their cultural contact, the French and Germans were developing mutually hostile attitudes, whereas the French and Russians, despite their sharply divergent ideological orientations, were characterizing each other in glowing terms. This was primarily because on the level of military power France and Germany considered each other hypothetical enemies, whereas Russia had a military alliance with France. The United States, the leading economic power already at that time—and the predominant cultural influence in the world, at least in material and popular culture—did not weigh much on the scale of international affairs because its armaments were limited and because it was not joined to any other power through a military alliance—another indication of the importance of military power as the determinant of international order.

It is therefore not surprising that Chinese-Japanese relations were ultimately determined by the power factor. Economic and cultural ties were growing, but they were not sufficiently influential to alter the overall power relationship. Japan was able to do what it did in China because, despite its economic underdevelopment and cultural dependence on China, it had succeeded in building up modern armed forces and came to be recognized as one of the major military powers, whereas China had not. If the main criterion for great-power status had been economic, China would have had as much claim to it as Japan; in fact Japan would not have counted as an economic power at all. If the criterion has been cultural, China surely would have been considered a greater power than Japan. The Japanese themselves in the Meiji era were inclined to think that their cultural role in the world was to serve as intermediaries between Western and Eastern civilizations or, more precisely, as transmitters of Western civilization to the East. Such a role by definition meant that Japan itself had little original to contribute. This point was made by the novelist Nagai Kafū who said that Meiji Japan had been avidly singing Western tunes but had been unable to develop its own song.[21] It remained to be seen whether in the wake of the World War, that unprecedented catastrophe that was an inevitable product of the nations' obsession with military power, when international order would inevitably have to be redefined, Japan would play a more active cultural role and, if so, how that would affect China's own transformation.

II

Culture

The primacy of power in Chinese-Japanese relations from the 1890s to the 1910s reflected a worldwide phenomenon. International affairs prior to the World War had been characterized by armaments, colonial rivalries, and military alliances far more than by commercial transactions or cultural interchanges. Although the latter activities had gone on among the major powers, they had not determined the structure and character of international relations. Economic and cultural ties between China and Japan had continued to deepen, but not in such a way as to alter the fundamental nature of the bilateral relationship that was one of a militarily superior power dominating a weaker neighbor.

The European war was a culmination of this trend toward the militarization of international affairs. And Japan's further encroachment on Chinese sovereignty during 1914–1918 was an aspect of the same story. But once the war ended, reaction set in. Europeans—and Americans as well, who also had firsthand experience of the war—began searching for a different definition of international relations so as never to repeat the mass slaughter that had depleted the West of close to ten million of its youths. Not surprisingly the survivors turned to economic and cultural ingredients. Some of them resurrected the traditional perception of commercial transactions among nations as the foundation of the postwar peace. That perception had been steadily undermined by a power-centered international system in which economic considerations had been subordinated to dictates of military calculations. In the aftermath of the war, however, with the former combatants trying to recover from war-inflicted destructions, economic objectives held center stage. Nations' economic interests too could clash, as was demonstrated most vividly by the European impasse on the German reparations question and the temporary occupation of the Ruhr region by French and Belgian troops. But by the mid-1920s a semblance of order in the international economic system had been restored, with some countries, led by the United States, returning to the gold standard and focusing their energies on industrialization and trade. There was an underlying assumption on the part of government and business leaders of the Western nations— and public officials and businessmen came to cooperate closely with one another in what historians have termed a "corporatist" arrangement of state-society collaboration— that this emphasis on economic transactions should serve to develop a world order more conducive to peace and interdependence than the prewar structure, which had been built on armed power. Because the United States was now the undisputed economic leader in the world, it was natural that Americans, led by men like Herbert Hoover and Thomas Lamont, should emerge as the epoch's most ardent spokesmen, advocates of an economic definition of international affairs. They visualized the use of America's resources, especially capital and technology, to create a world of interdependence where commercial ties would unite mankind, just as armaments and alliances once had divided them.

At the same time there also developed what may be called cultural internationalism, the view that more than anything else the world needed cultural activities among individuals and groups of different countries to help them develop some sort of global awareness that would transcend their narrow, selfish perspectives. This idea gained currency after the war, particularly among European intellectuals who, deeply disturbed by the wartime hysteria and ashamed of their own contribution to it, were convinced that the postwar international community must be built upon cosmopolitan cultural ties and outlooks. As Fritz Haber, the German physicist who helped found a German-Japanese institute for intellectual and scientific collaboration in the early 1920s, asserted, the destruction of Germany's military power showed that "our existence as a people depends on the maintenance of our intellectual great power position."[1] In other words, cultural achievements rather than armaments would now determine the greatness of nations and their fates. Peace would depend not on balances of military power but on cross-national interrelations at the intellectual level. Haber found many like-minded people, not only in Europe but in America and Asia as well, and some of them established international organizations to undertake joint scientific and other scholarly projects. They supported the League of Nations' efforts to promote communication among intellectuals of different countries in the strong belief that these enterprises would ensure a more stable and durable peace. So, in contrast to the period before 1914, it may be said that intellectuals and businessmen replaced generals and admirals as shapers and shakers of events. In *Heartbreak House,* a satirical play written during the war but not performed until peace had been established, George Bernard Shaw depicted the prewar separation of the spheres of "culture" from "power." Events had been defined and determined by men of "power," while people of "culture" watched hopelessly. Now it was the latter's turn to define the world.[2]

Chinese-Japanese relations after the First World War may be fitted into such a framework of changing definitions of international affairs. This does not mean that Japan's military superiority over and domination of China was reversed, or that the power-level relationship between the two nations disappeared. Far from it. So long as they remained national entities, part of their relationship would always be determined by military power. Indeed in the interwar years China's struggle to become a sovereign national entity inevitably, and once again, entailed military strengthening, a development with which the Japanese military came into conflict. Many of Japan's army and navy officers, rather than embracing new visions of world order, remained determined to hold on both to their privileged status at home and to the special position their military power had established on the continent. They grew increasingly alarmed at what appeared to be China's successful military strengthening and sought to cope with it through the use of force. While the overt employment of military force was somewhat limited during the 1920s, after 1931 it became virtually untamed. Clearly the Chinese-Japanese war which began that year and lasted till 1945 was first and foremost a military conflict, an aggressive war fought by Japanese soldiers and ultimately won by Chinese soldiers.

Merely to tell the story at the power level would be to isolate the bilateral relationship from the changing currents of international affairs and to assume that the postwar history of Chinese-Japanese relations was essentially a continuation of what had taken place before. Such an assumption would be tantamount to accepting uncritically the power definition of international affairs as always valid and, even more important, ignoring the profound transformations taking place in the two countries. For just as international affairs were becoming defined more and more by economic and cultural forces, inside both China and Japan these forces were asserting themselves to an unprecedented degree. Accordingly, Chinese-Japanese interactions in the interwar period, including even the 1930s, can best be understood as a fundamentally economic and cultural phenomenon rather than as a predominantly military one.

The year 1919 can be used to indicate the growing importance of the cultural factor in Chinese-Japanese relations, not only because of the May Fourth movement but also because it marked the beginning of a serious disarmament movement in postwar Japan. That year too, at the Paris peace conference, Chinese and Japanese delegates temporarily put aside their bitter dispute over Shantung (China had failed to dislodge Japan from the peninsula) and joined forces in pushing for the insertion of a race-equality clause in the covenant of the League of Nations. It seemed as though the postwar world, in the perception of Chinese and Japanese no less than of Europeans and Americans, would be comprehended and structured differently.

The May Fourth movement marked the beginning of a profound cultural transformation. Although the Chinese elites had always defined their country as a civilization rather than as a military power or an economic system, now the same stress on civilization entailed a different emphasis—one on democracy, science, literacy, language reform, and so forth that would redefine and, some argued, even destroy, traditional Chinese culture. Although the movement is usually put in the framework of awakened Chinese nationalism, it also should be viewed in the context of worldwide cultural awareness. In other words, there was as much internationalism as nationalism in the May Fourth phenomenon. Recall, for instance, the famous controversy between two leading intellectuals, Ch'en Tu-hsiu and Li

Ta-chao, on patriotism. Ch'en asserted that China as it existed during the Yüan Shih-k'ai period did not deserve to be an object of patriotism; only after the old China had been replaced by a democratic China, could the Chinese really feel a sense of affection for the nation. Li, on the other hand, argued that it was the patriotic duty of all Chinese to remake their country so that it could once again join the progress of civilization. Both Ch'en and Li, however, were looking at contemporary China from a universal viewpoint, the former as a stage in human evolution and the latter in a Hegelian conception of world history. It was these universalizing conceptions that made Chinese thought unique during the May Fourth era. China was to be seen as part of a global historical trend, and the country's existence was to be given significance in terms of international currents and developments. "We must make the world's life our own," wrote Li, "and realize that love of man is far more important than love of country."[3]

By calling on their countrymen to repudiate the old ways and to embrace universal themes like science and democracy as the new principles for ordering their society, Chinese intellectuals were echoing sentiments heard elsewhere in the world, Japan included. There too the new "world currents" emerging in the wake of the war were clearly recognized and served to link the so-called "Taishō democracy" (reform movements in the era of the Taishō emperor, 1912–1926) to the perceived global transformation. In January 1919 a writer for the influential monthly *Chūōkōron* (Central Review) noted that "global democratization" was the wave of the moment and that Japan should support this movement in China, Russia, and elsewhere.[4] To what extent such a sentiment was translated into active support for the May Fourth movement in China has not been explored by historians, but the term quoted and similar expressions found in several journals at that time suggest that at least a small handful of Japanese writers grasped the historic meaning of the Chinese movement from its inception and viewed it as part of the worldwide cultural redefinition, not just as an outraged nationalistic outburst against Japanese power. Japan's Taishō democracy and China's May Fourth movement, then, can be viewed as part of the same global phenomenon, an attempt to redefine the basis of national life and international affairs.

Although the conception was still rather vague, and although the Japanese soon would find that one strand at least of the May Fourth movement eventually came to take the form of national regeneration through military reunification and strengthening (undertaken by the combined forces of Sun Yat-sen's Kuomintang and the incipient Chinese Communist party) to which Japan's army would respond through the use of force, for the time being there was much interest in Japan in the redefining of the international order that was going on around the world after 1919. And one redefinition the Japanese supported, something into which they read much cultural significance, was disarmament. As *Tōyō keizai shinpô* (Oriental Economist), a major economic journal and a key organ of opinion for postwar internationalism, editorialized in 1919, there was no point in maintaining a large army since Germany had been defeated and since Russia, Japan's traditional hypothetical enemy, had gone through a democratic revolution and become peaceful. The United States, against which the Japanese navy had developed war plans, now, according to the disarmament advocates, exemplified peace and democracy so that there was no cause to fear war between the two countries so long as Japan did not persist in its militaristic activities in China.[5]

Thus reasoning, Taishō intellectuals—at least some of the most outspoken ones—sought to redefine Japan's foreign relations. Like their counterparts elsewhere, they asserted that the old system of international affairs based on armaments and colonies was giving way to one characterized by peace and democracy. Instead of armament rivalries and colonial competition, henceforth the nations of the world would deal with one another commercially and culturally, stressing industry, transportation, education, and other nonmilitary pursuits. The success of the Washington disarmament conference (1921–1922) was most encouraging to Japan's reformers, for it seemed to indicate that by renouncing their naval rivalry the great powers were expressing readiness to base their interrelations on other foundations.

This suggests that there was a conjunction of forces in both China and Japan looking for a new definition of national and international affairs. It was symbolic that at the Paris peace conference China and Japan called for a race-equality principle in the League covenant. If the new world order were to emphasize peace and communication rather than conflict and misunderstanding, it made sense to start by having the principle accepted as a core value of postwar international relations. That the Western powers were not yet ready to agree to it came as a shock to Asians and turned some of them, including a few Japanese intellectuals, into advocates of anti-Westernism, championing the cause, as they said, of liberating the colored races from white domination.[6] While such views were not yet widely shared, the quest for race equality was not an isolated phenomenon at the time. Anticolonial struggles in such areas as India and Indochina were gathering momentum, and their spokesmen believed the movement would be given a tremendous boost by the coming of what appeared to be a new world order.

Ho Chi Minh was only one of many Asian nationalists who equated the Versailles peace with the beginning of a novel phase of the colonial liberation movement.[7] Although the race-equality proposal and the struggle for Asian self-determination did not bear immediate fruit, they underlined the growing importance of nonpower factors in international affairs. Earlier the domination of the Western powers over colored peoples had been taken for granted; even Japan had identified its position with that of the West. Race antagonisms had existed, but, as could be seen in Japanese relations with the United States, they had not been allowed to affect the basic structure of interpower relations. Now, as the power component was losing its preeminent status in the postwar world, other factors, of which race was a conspicuous example, were asserting themselves.

Chinese-Japanese relations during the 1920s can be understood in such a framework. These relations were determined far more by economic and cultural than by military forces. Military power of course continued to define one aspect of the bilateral relationship. But compared with the preceding decade, not to mention the one that followed, on the whole the 1920s were characterized by the absence of large-scale direct military confrontation between the two countries or Japan's blatantly aggressive designs to control China. It is easy to dismiss such a development as a temporary phenomenon, a mere lull in an otherwise tumultuous relationship in the framework of Japan's military domination of China. To do so, however, would be to dismiss as of little consequence some significant developments in the two countries that would not fit neatly into such a framework. Japanese military power was actually retrenched during the 1920s, the army scrapping two of its divisions and the navy agreeing to the disarmament formula worked out at the Washington conference. These measures served to reduce Japan's defense expenditures from 731 million yen in 1921—the highest figure since the Meiji Restoration—to less than half a billion yen by 1930, a reduction of nearly 40 percent.

Such an abrupt reversal deserves to be given due consideration in any discussion of Japanese foreign affairs after the war. To be sure, Japan was not alone in undertaking arms control; because other countries were also doing so, the nation still remained one of the major military powers in the postwar world. The crucial fact is, however, that the ratio of arms spending in Japan after 1921 fell to below 5 percent of the national income for the first time in its modern history. This was a decade when government expenditures too remained relatively low, claiming less than 16 percent of the national income, and defense expenditures likewise accounted for a smaller portion of annual budgets than had been the case before the war. In other words, there was a clear shift in Japanese policy, away from the building up of military force and the maintenance of balance-of-power considerations to one of retrenchment and arms-control agreements. The abrogation of the one military alliance that had been a key to Japanese strategy, the Anglo-Japanese alliance, in 1921, was thus quite symbolic. Henceforth Japanese security would hinge less on these traditional instruments than on international cooperation and goodwill.

The army and the navy did not disappear of course, but their reduced forces were considered adequate for the purpose of protecting the homeland and the colonial possessions. They would not be sufficient for carrying out more aggressive undertakings. We may concede that the two expeditions to Shantung, in 1927 and 1928, were aggressive acts of the traditional sort; troops were dispatched to protect

Japanese nationals in the way of the Chinese Nationalists' "northern expedition." Moreover, the second Shantung expedition coincided with a plot by the Kwantung army to assassinate Chang Tso-lin, the Manchurian warlord, as he fled the Peking-Tientsin area by train in the face of the advancing Nationalist forces. Chang's assassination, which its plotters carried out in order to prevent his return to the Northeastern Provinces (Manchuria) and to create confusion in the region, clearly was designed to frustrate the Nationalists' attempt to unify the whole country, including these provinces. Thus indirectly pitting Chinese and Japanese military forces, the incident was a harbinger of things to come in the 1930s.

Nevertheless, these incidents were significant because only a small number of troops were involved, and in the two Shantung affairs the expeditionary forces were withdrawn within several weeks. Even more important, there was a public outcry in Japan against the expeditions, and in the case of Chang Tso-lin's assassination the emperor himself let his extreme displeasure be known. He reprimanded Prime Minister Tanaka Giichi, a former army general, for his irresoluteness in punishing those responsible for the offence. This was a rare instance in modern Japanese history when the emperor virtually single-handedly brought about the resignation of a prime minister because the latter seemed to have acted contrary to established policy.[8] These events suggest that military and power-political considerations were no longer being allowed free play but had to adapt to the developing climate of opinion that was much less generous to the power-definition of national affairs than earlier.

In such an atmosphere it is not surprising that some Japanese even began questioning the wisdom of holding on to its colonial empire. Best known was Ishibashi Tanzan, the editor of *Tōyō keizai shinpō,* who advocated what he called "little Japan-ism," or a strategy for a smaller Japan. According to this plan, Japan would be well advised to give up its formal empire in Korea, Taiwan, and parts of China (especially Manchuria) and concentrate on trade and other economic dealings with the neighboring peoples. Yanaibara Tadao, a young economist who occupied the chair of colonial policy studies at the Tokyo Imperial University, openly questioned the justice of retaining the rights and privileges in Manchuria. These were minority viewpoints, and few were willing to go that far. Nitobe Inazō, a leading "internationalist" of the period, never saw any contradiction between the Japanese policies of international cooperation and disarmament, on one hand, and the retention of the colonial empire, on the other. After all, most other nations still had colonies; besides, Nitobe wrote, Taiwanese, Koreans, and Chinese were not yet fully ready for independence.[9] That would seem to have been a more typical view, even of the internationalists in Japan during the 1920s. Still, it is significant that anti-imperialistic and antimilitaristic views were expressed more or less freely at that time, something that must be understood in the context of the worldwide ethos against war and militarism.

Without this ethos the Japanese might have exercised less restraint in China. For China, if anything, was even more fragmented and militarily weaker during most of the 1920s than in the 1910s. In the absence of a centralized authority, warlords continued to control subdivisions of the country. Most of them had been trained as modern military officers during the waning years of the Ch'ing dynasty, but instead of jointly forming the core of a national army, they tended to organize their own units, ruling over certain regions and entering into temporary alliances with one another to augment further their power positions. Individually the warlords were skilled warriors, adept at training the men under them; but this did not add up to national military power. Yet because Japan and other nations tended to refrain from overtly intervening in Chinese affairs, this situation did not prove to be ruinous for the country and may even have facilitated the tasks of the revolutionaries. If the warlords had united against the Nationalist and Communist forces, the latter might have found it much more difficult to succeed. As it was, they were able to pit the warlords against one another and even to obtain the allegiance of some of them for the revolutionary movement.

Initially at least, although they fully understood the need to develop a revolutionary army to unify the country, the revolutionaries were fundamentally not a military force but an ideological one. The Kuomintang under Sun Yat-sen had its own armed force. It was centered in the Whampoa Military Academy, which was headed by Chiang Kai-shek after his return from a short visit to the Soviet Union (to seek that country's assistance). But that alone would not have enabled the revolutionaries to seize power. There were few military campaigns between the forces of the revolutionaries and the warlords; rather, the former used diplomacy, propaganda, and indoctrination to bring the latter into their fold. First the so-called southern militarists, those who had emerged independent of the northern warlords who had ties with the old Peiyang army, and then those in the central provinces became steadily incorporated into the revolutionary army through indoctrination campaigns led by political representatives dispatched by the Kuomintang. That one of the major warlords, Feng Yü-hsiang, joined the Kuomintang in 1926 was a symbolic development in that it pointed to the possibility of coalescing various Chinese factions into a unified army through propaganda.

In a sense, then, the triumph of the revolutionary movement was a victory of ideology over conventional military power, another reflection of one important characteristic of the postwar world. By 1928, in any event, an ideologically driven, modern army had come into existence in China, although it did not totally replace warlord armies and it would itself not be free from centrifugal tendencies. Still, within ten years after the May Fourth movement began, a China with a modern armed force imbued with the spirit of 1919 had emerged. The Japanese army, for its part, recognized the development's significance, which was why some of its leaders supported military expeditions to Shantung. Nevertheless, they refrained from more extensive interference, a circumstance that was quite fortunate from the Chinese point of view.

The Nationalist unification of China in 1928 was made possible in part by the changed international circumstances of the period. To the extent that after 1919 the world was characterized by a diminished emphasis on military power, this was precisely the opportune moment for the Chinese to undertake their own military unification. Ironically their very success was to provoke Japan's response in kind. Once the international context that restrained military behavior began to erode in the 1930s, the situation inevitably brought about a frontal clash between Chinese and Japanese forces.

Before we discuss that phase of Chinese-Japanese military relations, however, it is important to consider the crucial developments in the economic and cultural spheres during the 1920s. Economically postwar China and Japan became even more interdependent than before. As Japan began to emphasize nonmilitary objectives of its national policy, it was natural that concerted efforts should have been made to promote trade and other economic activities abroad. But there were particular reasons why China was of critical importance. Japanese trade had reached a stage where the share of manufactured goods had caught up with primary products such as tea and silk in overall exports. This reflected the quickening tempo of industrialization that had been given impetus by the European war. The number of factories employing more than five laborers nearly doubled between 1914 and 1929, as did the number of the total work force employed in manufacturing. Close to five million, of a total population of sixty million, were employed in factories, in contrast to fourteen million engaged in agriculture. The country was not as industrialized as Western Europe or the United States, but Japan was fast moving in that direction. The situation was reflected in trade figures, where during most of the 1920s the combined total of exports and imports exceeded 4 billion yen a year, or about 30 percent of the national income. Imports always exceeded exports, as the country had to import foodstuffs and raw materials. In order to remedy the situation it was all the more important to expand export trade in manufactured items. That could only mean the growing importance of the China market.

During the 1920s Japan replaced Britain as the leading trading nation in China. Even as late as the early 1920s, Britain's share in the China trade was more than 40 percent, higher than any other country's. But this changed after 1925, the year of the May Thirtieth movement, which resulted in the Chinese boycotting of British goods and ships in retaliation against the shooting of strikers in Shanghai and elsewhere. The movement particularly affected the trade between Hong Kong and China as the boycott spread to the Crown colony and some Chinese demonstrators were killed at Canton in June. Overall British imports to China fell to 30 percent of the total. In contrast, that year saw Japan's share reaching 30 percent for the first time, and in 1926 and 1927 Japanese trade in China exceeded British. Considering the fact that China's overall trade nearly doubled between 1919 and 1929, this was a significant achievement and indicated that China had become even more critical to Japan's industrializing economy than ever before. In 1929, for instance, Japan's total exports amounted to 2,218 million yen, of which 525 million, or close to one-fourth, went to China. The United States was still the most important market for Japanese exports, but China was fast catching up—or so it seemed. Because Japan was selling mostly primary products such as silk and silk goods to the United States, it could be expected that China, which was purchasing larger and larger quantities of Japanese cotton textiles and machinery, would prove to be the key to a successful economic transformation of Japan.

Given such a situation, it is not surprising that the tariff question, rather than military episodes like expeditions to Shantung or the assassination of Chang Tso-lin, proved to be the most seriously contested issue between the two countries during the 1920s—a clear indication of the crucial role played by economic affairs. This became evident during the Peking tariff conference of 1925–1926, convened as a result of an international agreement signed at the Washington conference and designed to help China increase its tariff revenue. All powers, including Japan, recognized that the customs receipts under the old treaties—nominally 5 percent ad valorem but in reality as low as 2.5 percent on average—were wholly inadequate to meet Chinese governmental expenses, and therefore that ways must be found to augment them through the imposition of a customs surtax, to be levied in addition to the prevailing treaty tariff. Japan wanted to keep such a surtax as low as possible, 2.5 percent at most, while other nations were willing to agree to higher rates. This was because it was felt that Japanese goods, especially cotton textiles, would not be able to compete with indigenous Chinese products if they were subject to substantially increased import duties, whereas other countries were exporting commodities for which there were few Chinese substitutes. Negotiations were endless, Japan maintaining its adamant opposition to higher rates, but in the end a compromise was struck: a variable import schedule, ranging from 2.5 to 22.5 percent, was established. Japan accepted it since most Japanese goods came under the lower categories. The agreement, however, was not implemented immediately because of political turmoil in China. The adjournment of the tariff conference coincided with the launching of the northern expedition by the revolutionaries, so for the period 1926–1928 there was no central authority in China to which the foreign nations could assign the increased tariff revenue.

The story did not end there. Once the Nationalists came to power in 1928, one of their first goals was to resolve the customs issue—not only through the implementation of the surtax agreement but by an outright restoration of tariff autonomy to China. Their argument was straightforward: no self-respecting nation—and China was at last emerging as one—would do without such autonomy, one of the sovereign rights of a modern state. In fact, at the Paris peace conference the Chinese delegation already had declared that national sovereignty consisted of territorial integrity, political independence, and economic autonomy. Although nei-

ther the country's territorial integrity nor its political independence was as yet self-evident, all factions in China were
united on the tariff question, even during the period of warlordism and internecine struggles. Not only would tariff
autonomy free the nation from foreign control of its trade,
it would also provide those in power a stable source of
revenue with which to govern. For merchants and manufacturers increases in import duties would protect domestic
industry. As a Kuomintang declaration asserted in 1927,
despite the enormous size of China, its economy was in a
sorry state because the treaty tariffs had discouraged the
growth of manufacturing. The regaining of tariff autonomy, combined with the abolition of likin and other transit
taxes, should enable the nation to undertake rapid economic
growth.[10] Thus one of the first things the Nationalist government did when it captured Peking in 1928 was to call
upon the powers to negotiate new treaties of commerce to
replace the old unequal treaties. In the meantime, it would
implement the graduated customs surtaxes that had been
agreed to at the Peking tariff conference. It is noteworthy
that when this was done, in 1929, customs receipts increased
more than threefold. It could easily be expected that once
tariff autonomy was regained, even more revenue would be
collected.

Once again Japan dragged its feet. It was the last of the
major powers to grant tariff autonomy to China. The Western powers were much more willing to accede to the Chinese demand, reasoning that because tariff autonomy had
become a symbol of national sovereignty, they should be
ready to grant it to China and then to enter into mutually
advantageous customs agreements to protect their trade.
Japanese officials, on the other hand, concerned that the new
Nanking regime might begin imposing higher duties on
Japan's imports, argued that the grant of tariff autonomy to

China must be preceded by negotiations for a new trade agreement between the two countries. It was not until May 1930, nearly two years after most other countries had done so, that Japan finally agreed to Chinese tariff autonomy. This was coupled with an agreement that certain categories of Japanese imports would be subjected to relatively lower customs rates. Even this was not enough to satisfy the Japanese, for they insisted upon, and obtained from a reluctant China, a promise that the latter would set aside 5 million tael each year from the customs receipts to repay foreign debts.

The question of foreign debt was part of the larger picture of China's financial dependence on other countries. Like other powers, though initially on a much more modest scale, Japan had shipped capital to China in the form of investments and loans. Japanese investment in Chinese railways and factories had grown steadily, and by the 1920s they had become profitable operations. The South Manchuria Railway, for instance, was earning a revenue of 185 million yen in 1923, an amount larger than the ordinary budget for Korea of 101 million yen or for Taiwan of 100 million yen.[11] By the mid-1920s Japanese cotton-spinning and -weaving factories in Shanghai were thriving; despite occasional labor disputes, the total number of their spindles (over one million) surpassed those of British factories. In 1930 Japanese textile factories in Shanghai were capitalized at over 120 million yen. Employing more than 58,000 Chinese workers, these mills were making substantial profits since their products could be marketed in China and compete successfully with indigenous Chinese manufactures. For that very reason these enterprises were resented by Chinese nationalists, who yearned to regain foreign railway and manufacturing concessions as well as tariff autonomy. But little could be done in the absence of a comprehensive national strategy for economic development, which would be worked out only during the 1930s.

Quite apart from such investments was the even thornier question of foreign loans to succeeding Chinese governments, going back to the French-Russian loans to Peking in the immediate aftermath of the Chinese-Japanese war. Millions of dollars had been lent to the Ch'ing dynasty and its successor regimes. Some of these loans had been secured on customs receipts, some on other sources of government revenue. From the viewpoint of foreign lenders, these were legitimate financial transactions that should be honored by the Nationalists if they claimed to be the new government of China. For their part, the Nationalists looked upon foreign debts as a legacy of imperialism and warlordism, something for which the Chinese people were not responsible. Arguing this case just as ardently as their counterparts did in Mexico, the Soviet Union, and elsewhere, the Nationalist leaders insisted that such political loans were invalid, and did not have to be honored. But matters could not simply be left at that for the simple reason that foreigners would insist on debt repayment. So long as the issue remained unresolved, it would be very difficult for the new Chinese government to raise money abroad, which it needed to consolidate its position in the country and to undertake a faster economic transformation than had been possible during years of domestic turmoil. The actual amount the government (or rather its predecessors) owed foreigners was not extraordinary; as of 1929, external obligations totaled some 45 million yuan. Because several times this amount was collected by the customs administration that year, it should not have been excessively difficult to set aside a portion of import duties each year to repay the foreign debt.

The problem was that, in addition to various loans secured on customs receipts and other kinds of public funds, the central government as well as the provinces in the early Republican period had contracted many so-called unsecured loans, most of which were of Japanese origin, including the Nishihara loans of 1918 given to the Chinese Ministry of Communications which amounted to 354 million tael. There was tremendous resistance to honoring such obligations, which were viewed by the Chinese, with justification, as political loans. But in the end the Nationalist authorities agreed at least to reexamine each unsecured loan with a view to settling all foreign debts ultimately. The decision was part of Nanking's overall orientation of its foreign affairs at the end of the 1920s and the beginning of the 1930s, when it was anxious to reincorporate China into the international community. Because that community was characterized more by economic interdependence than by military rivalries, China's new tariff autonomy, coupled with steps taken toward debt settlement, fitted into the picture very nicely.

By then, Japan too had come to accommodate itself to the emergence of China as an economically modernizing nation whose basic sovereign rights had to be respected. Shidehara Kijūrō, foreign minister during 1924–1927 and again during 1929–1931, called this accommodation the policy of "coexistence and coprosperity." He drove hard bargains with the Chinese regarding tariff and debt matters, but he was opposed to the use of force to protect or promote Japan's economic interests in China. It was precisely because he eschewed the military alternative that he felt he had to push very hard in negotiating advantageous trade and debt agreements. And by and large he was satisfied that the various agreements that the two governments had successfully negotiated by 1931 would promote East Asian "coprosperity."

Ultimately coprosperity would have to entail interpersonal ties, a relationship of mutual respect and trust between individual Chinese and Japanese. How much of this was there in the 1920s? Did the earlier tenuous cultural connections between the two peoples grow after the First World War? Or did such ties remain submerged under the larger themes of power and economic relations?

The picture is mixed. It would be correct to say that during the 1920s more Chinese and Japanese civilians came into contact with one another than ever before. This was particularly true in Shanghai, where Japanese-owned cotton textile mills employed tens of thousands of Chinese workers. Relations between them and their Japanese employers were not always happy, as attested to by the fact that even prior to May 1925, when anti-British boycotts flared up all over China, some 30,000 Chinese workers at Japanese factories in the city struck, demanding better working conditions and protesting the way they were treated by Japanese supervisors. The strikes led to Japanese concessions on working conditions, but in return the Japanese insisted on China's honoring contractual obligations. The tense atmosphere persisted throughout the remainder of the decade and might have become even more critical had not the Nationalists, after 1927, begun reining in labor movements. In the context of cultural relations, however, the important point is that the joining of Japanese capital and technology with Chinese labor was viewed in both countries as a better way to define their relations than an emphasis on Japanese military presence on Chinese soil. Japanese factories in China symbolized the degree to which the idea of coprosperity might become a reality.

A more straightforward attempt at promoting Chinese-Japanese cultural relations was made in 1922, when the Japanese government decided to remit the unpaid portion of the Boxer indemnity, about 7.7 million pounds (of the initial 10 million), to China to be used for cultural activities. The United States had taken the lead in this direction, using some of the indemnity funds to bring Chinese students to America. Now belatedly the Japanese, as well as most European countries, were following suit. In 1923 the Foreign Ministry established a division of Chinese cultural affairs with a view to regularizing student exchanges. Initially it was determined that a maximum of 320 Chinese students would be selected and brought over to Japan, their living expenses to be borne by the ministry. They were joined by hundreds, perhaps thousands, of others who went to Japan to study. Their number was probably larger than comparable figures elsewhere.

A portion of the Boxer funds was set aside for the establishment of Tōyō Bunka Kenyūjo, the Institute for the Study of Oriental Culture, which was to be affiliated with the Tokyo Imperial University and promote scholarly research on contemporary China. This was as significant a step as the student exchanges, for the study of contemporary China was still in its embryonic stages in Japan. Japanese scholars continued to concentrate on classical Chinese literature and philosophy, and few were interested in turning to contemporary China as an object of scholarly inquiry. Those who sought to do so tended to come under the influence of Western scholarship, particularly Marxism. In 1929 a group of Japanese Marxists organized an association for the study of Chinese problems, but they followed Comintern guidelines closely, and what they examined was not so much China as Soviet perspectives on the Chinese revolution. Parenthetically, even the Marxists still referred to China as "Shina," although by then the term had come to express, in the eyes of Chinese, Japan's contempt for its neighbor. In 1930 the Nationalist government officially protested against the use of this term in formal communications from Tokyo, and Japan duly obliged, agreeing to call China, Chūka Minkoku (the same characters as the Chinese name for their country, "Chung-hua Min-kuo") in official language. This change apparently aroused much controversy in Japan, with letters to the editors of newspapers arguing pro and con. The episode, admittedly a small incident, was yet another example of the new relationship which was involving wider dimensions and more numerous circles of people than before.[12]

Studies by Joshua Fogel, Sophie Lee, and others have unearthed the presence of various Japanese living in China at that time, pursuing their own cultural activities. Nakae Ushikichi was a recluse, carrying on research into ancient Chinese society and totally critical of Japan's military presence in China. His friends and associates, many of them now forgotten, were mostly Chinese. There may have been other Nakaes who developed networks of interpersonal relationships that added up to another story of Chinese-Japanese relations than the usual picture of power and economic relations. One such network centered on Hashikawa Tokio, a scholar-journalist who was a close friend of Li Ta-chao, Hu Shih, and others. In 1923 he became director of the Peking Humanities Institute, an organization established in 1927 to promote collaborative scholarly undertakings. Many Chinese who cooperated with Hashikawa, Sophie Lee notes, "reasoned that culture and politics were two distinct entities."[13] While condemning Japanese military presence or criticizing Japanese foreign policy, they believed that cultural pursuits had their own raison d'être. It is difficult to ascertain how many Chinese or Japanese in the 1920s shared such views or cooperated in joint cultural undertakings. Their number or its significance should not be exaggerated, but neither should they be ignored or dismissed altogether.

The deepening literary ties between China and Japan at this time are another case in point. Though the phenomenon has not been studied systematically, the atmosphere of cultural renovation or revolution in both countries after 1919 was conducive to encouraging direct encounters by poets, novelists, and artists. Young Chinese imbued with the spirit of the May Fourth movement met young Japanese spearheading Taishō democracy, and they often collaborated in experimenting with new forms of literary expression. What was then called the "new romanticism," exalting individual emotions and obsessed with personal agonies, attracted some of them; others became devotees of esperanto, the new language that would, it was widely hoped, bring internationalism and freedom. For some Chinese visitors to Japan, like the novelist T'ien Han, the modern theater of Taishō Japan was an inspiration, while a considerable number of well-known Japanese writers, such as Tanizaki Jun'ichirō and Akutagawa Ryūnosuke, went to China, not in connection with a war or a political event, but simply to see the neighboring country at first hand. Their observations of contemporary China were not always flattering, but it is worth noting that both they and their Chinese counterparts who went to Japan were primarily interested in culture rather than politics or economics. It is said that T'ien Han saw over one hundred movies in Tokyo; this became the basis of his later work as director of the film department of the Nanking government. If, as the American sociologist Robert Park remarked in the late 1920s, the cinema was "the symbol of a new dimension of our international and racial relations which is neither economic nor political, but cultural," then the experiences of T'ien Han and countless others could be said to have been very much part of the worldwide phenomenon.[14] Ultimately the cultural pursuits and the new awareness of the ties that bound Chinese and Japanese, and others as well, might have contributed to solidifying forces for internationalism and against militarism and war. Such, unfortunately, was not to be, but the tragic story of the 1930s can be fully understood only when put in the context of the intensification of cultural associations in the preceding decade.

If anything, it could even be argued that cultural forces never abated in the 1930s but became distorted, twisted to define national and international affairs in ways never anticipated by the promoters of cultural connections during the 1920s. Ideally, as China and Japan became increasingly interconnected economically and culturally, while the latter's aggressive militarism was held in check, the two peoples should have developed a more stable and peaceful relationship than ever before. In reality of course Chinese-Japanese relations after 1931 were anything but stable or peaceful. The decade saw naked Japanese aggression, atrocities, and destructiveness at the expense of China, where millions were killed, maimed, and humiliated. Did these phenomena not indicate that military force and calculations were once again predominant, that economic and cultural affairs came to be subordinated to the cold dictates of an aggressive war?

The answer to such questions can only be yes, but to end there would be to leave unexplored many important questions for the meaning of the 1930s. Why did power considerations once again come to dominate Japan's approach to China? Did the reassertion of the power factor mean that Chinese-Japanese relations had returned to where they were before 1919, or did they evolve in different ways this time? What happened to economic and cultural forces during the long war between the two countries that began in 1931? Were they complementary to, collaborative with, or subversive of military calculations? Finally, did the new developments in Chinese-Japanese relations reflect trends elsewhere? Just as global conditions once had provided the setting for certain characteristics of Chinese-Japanese relations, did the world of the 1930s define the nature of the bilateral relationship?

These extremely important questions cannot be dealt with extensively here. I shall, instead, focus on issues related to the cultural dimension during the 1930s. First, however, the power and economic aspects of Chinese-Japanese relations should be briefly outlined. The story of Chinese-Japanese military relations in that period involved Japan's use of force to try to establish control over China. By 1939 it had succeeded in the Northeastern Provinces, Inner Mongolia, and northern China, as well as the major cities and railways in the rest of the country. The Chinese resisted the Japanese conquerors both through their own military efforts and through foreign assistance. By the end of the decade it was becoming evident that Japan would never be able to conquer the whole of China and that the latter would become part of a coalition of nations to resist aggression. In the end China would be united with the United States, Britain, the Soviet Union, and others against Japan, which would align itself with Germany and Italy. The ensuing war would result in the complete defeat and destruction of the latter.

The military conflict had serious economic connotations for both China and Japan. For China the war meant having to divert its resources away from domestic economic reconstruction. Prior to the Manchurian incident, the country under the Nationalists had made plans for industrialization, trade expansion, efficient tax collection, and other programs to modernize the economy, but increasingly the resources of the country would have to be devoted to military use. The situation was exacerbated by the world economic crisis, which drastically reduced volumes and values of trade. Nevertheless, by the mid-1930s, coinciding with a lull in the military conflict with Japan, the Chinese economy had begun to regain its vitality. A British advisory group led by Frederick Leith-Ross helped Nanking undertake financial reforms, decoupling the monetary system from silver and introducing a new currency, fapi, which was linked to the pound-sterling. Tax collection, at least from areas outside of the northern provinces, improved, and the Nationalist authorities began an ambitious project of building the infrastructure. It is possible to argue that China was economically healthier in July 1937, on the eve of the resumption of full-scale fighting with Japan, than it had been since the late Ch'ing period.

The picture for Japan was not very different. That nation too had been hit by the worldwide Depression, although the impact there was much more limited than it was on more advanced industrial countries like the United States and Germany. Japan's unemployment, for instance, was less than 500,000 in the early 1930s, in contrast to Germany's six million or America's ten million. The quick military successes in Manchuria proved to be an economic catalyst, putting an end even to this degree of unemployment and enabling Japan to recover from its brief recession. By 1932 its industrial output was back where it had been in 1927, the first year of the recession, and national income reached an unprecedented height of 14 billion yen in 1935, or about 200 yen per capita. Trade too resumed its expansion, with Japanese exports in 1936 amounting to 2,693 million yen, the highest figure up to that point. Imports, however, exceeded exports, and this continued throughout the decade. Nevertheless, the average Japanese enjoyed a higher standard of living—though it was quite modest compared with that of even Depression-inflicted Western countries—than ever before.

Things began to change for both China and Japan after the Marco Polo Bridge incident of July 7, 1937, ushering in an eight-year-long war. Both nations mobilized their resources for war, sacrificing peacetime programs to military needs. China's devastation was immediately visible in Nanking, Hankow, Canton, and other cities where civilians as well as combatants were killed, property was destroyed, and severe shortages of goods caused skyrocketing inflations. China's loss, however, did not translate into Japan's gain. The Japanese too found the costs of war prohibitive. Military expenditures again exceeded 40 percent of annual budgets, or more than 20 percent of the national income. Trade deficits vis-à-vis areas outside of Asia (particularly the United States) increased because Japan's war machine needed military aircraft and vehicles, ships, petroleum, and other necessities not obtainable within the now enlarged empire.

The war did not make much sense economically to the Japanese, not to mention the Chinese—unless they somehow perceived the war as a prelude to an economic union that would benefit both countries. This was one type of rationalization Japan used in explaining the disastrous war. But to fight an economically disastrous war in order to unite the two economies (or what was left of them) was an absurd proposition. If economic union were the primary objective, diplomacy, not war, should have been resorted to. So purely economic considerations were of secondary importance, at least after 1937. This is another way of saying that the economic dimension of Chinese-Japanese relations lost its autonomy. I could simplify this and say that the economic dimension became subordinated to the power dimension, or that the gap between power and economics widened significantly.

That of course was a reflection of the larger international picture. The most obvious contrast between the period just prior to the outbreak of the Second World War and that leading up to the First World War is that the former was an era of the worst economic crisis of modern times, whereas the latter was a period of unprecedented prosperity. Before 1914 a stable international economic system had been established, whereas after 1929 no comparable system existed. The powers that went to war in 1914 could "afford" to do so, whereas those that fought after 1939, with the exception of the United States, were economically far less prepared to wage total war. The relationship between power and economics had changed drastically, even though in both cases the fact that war came meant that by definition the power factor asserted its primacy.

All such considerations seem to point to the importance of bringing in the third, cultural, factor into the discussion. Why did power assert primacy in both instances, despite sharply contrasting economic situations? One could adopt a crude power determinism and say that power is always primary. But that only begs the question. Why is power always primary? Rather than accepting such an assertion as a given, it will be more useful to link it to the cultural dimension of international affairs. In the preceding chapter

I suggested that power and culture were often in an antagonistic relationship in Chinese-Japanese relations before the First World War; Japan's cultural indebtedness to China did not prevent its military assertiveness on the continent. The cultural dimension here served as a potential check upon Japan's military dominance by reminding the Japanese that, culturally, the Chinese were superior in many respects and that in that realm the two peoples had much to contribute to each other.

What role did culture play in the 1930s? Did it function as a check on Japanese aggression or did it reinforce it? Did it confirm the primacy of power over economics or was it a bridge between the power and economic dimensions of Chinese-Japanese relations?

These questions provide one way of examining those relations during the 1930s. A good point of departure for discussing the cultural dimension may be found in an observation made by Janet Flanner, an American journalist who lived in Paris during most of the interwar years. Writing in 1939, on the eve of the Second World War, she remarked, "Maybe Europe is in for a Hundred Years' Peace, like the Hundred Years' War, and looking much the same—years of threats, conquests that are small measured against the disruption of men's minds, peace in the manner of war and with almost the same costs, until everybody goes bankrupt from being so well armed that nobody dares fight the big fight."[15] Although this last statement was to prove wrong, Flanner grasped one essential characteristic of European affairs in the 1930s: the juxtaposition of war and peace. Nations behaved as though they were preparing for war, and yet before 1940 no full-scale fighting took place. It was a state neither of peace nor of war; perhaps we could say that it was a state where peace and war existed simultaneously.

Although the same could not be said of Asia, where there was no mistaking that war existed between China and Japan, it is possible to discover beneath the surface activities and developments not altogether connected with the war and oriented toward other objectives: in the case of Japan, desperate attempts to persuade the Chinese to accept a compromise peace; for the latter, a serious effort at national rebuilding. These and other phenomena did not hide the odiousness of Japanese aggression and atrocities, but even these were often cloaked in a rhetoric other than of war and violence. Perhaps, paraphrasing Flanner, one might say that in Asia there was "war in the manner of peace." In one respect moreover her astute observation applied equally to Europe and Asia: what she termed "the disruption of men's minds."

This, or what might today be called moral uncertainty, intellectual confusion, or the disappearance of a familiar sense of order bespoke a state of affairs in which culture in the sense of shared symbols or structures of meaning was in disarray. For that very reason, paradoxically, much was said about culture. Perhaps it was a way to reestablish new certainty, to provide a sense of community when the customary networks of cohesive relations had disappeared.

This can be seen in many aspects of international relations in the 1930s. Because of the Depression, economic forces no longer functioned as normal regulators of world affairs, and "the disruption of men's minds" made it difficult for culture to replace economics in carrying out the task. This might have left power as the most obvious determinant of international relations. One fascinating aspect of the 1930s, however, is that it did not quite work out that way. Various manifestations of culture affected the ways in which power operated. Moral ambiguities and intellectual confusion might create a situation where national leaders would decide to use struggle and war as the means of generating social harmony and cohesiveness. Or psychological revulsion against any type of collective action, including war, might be so strong that all such attempts might fail. In reality these contradictory tendencies might even exist in the same country. Eyewitness accounts of Nazi Germany show that war-weariness existed side by side with anticipation of war.[16] The same phenomenon could be detected in the democracies. The simultaneous existence of war and peace, or power and culture, could be seen in the widespread awareness in the 1930s that international and national affairs were inseparable. Power in the sense of geopolitical calculations and culture in the sense of domestic societal orientations were intertwined to such an unprecedented degree that there could be no such thing as a purely foreign war. A war would signal domestic transformation, just as internal developments would make war a likely, or an unlikely, proposition. What George Orwell called "political war" on the basis of his experiences in the Spanish Civil War perhaps best describes the phenomenon. Domestic transformation has always been a key factor to be taken into consideration when nations contemplate external conflicts. At the same time war would be justified not simply in traditional terms, as a defense of national independence, honor, or interests, but also in terms of what it did to restructure the society, to redefine culture.

In some such fashion, culture operated differently in the 1930s than it had in the 1920s. The primacy of culture and economics in one decade had established the primacy of peace over war. Now, with economics losing its decisiveness, power and culture were juxtaposed, signaling the simultaneous existence of war and peace. War as peace, and peace as war—this was the picture of the 1930s. Economics somehow disappeared from this equation, not to be rediscovered until the postwar world.

The intricate intertwining of culture and power may be seen even in Japan's naked aggression in China after 1931. The conquest of Manchuria, although it was a straightforward and conventional development in which a nation undertook to extend areas under its military control, had other implications. The Japanese conquerors, while they entrenched their military power in the Northeastern Provinces, began couching the event in broader terms in order to imply its relevance to social transformation at home as well as in these provinces. The Japanese encountered ethnic diversity in this region and determined to use it as the basis of a vision of the new empire. Japanese propagandists, such as those who organized the Kyōwakai (Concordia Society), asserted that their aim was to establish a harmonious relationship among all five races—Han Chinese, Mongols, Manchus, Koreans, and Japanese—in Manchuria so that together they might contribute to the welfare of the whole world. The idea was ludicrous in view of what actually took place, but at least the propagandists did not follow the German or Italian racial policies. Even as late as 1940 leaflets explaining Kyōwakai ideals emphasized that they differed from Nazism or fascism because of their lack of race prejudice, particularly anti-Semitism.[17] The self-conscious doctrine of race harmony, rather than innate race antagonism, seems to have reflected the interest on the part of those who controlled Manchuria—the Kwantung army, the South Manchuria Railway, and others—in doing something to create a unique setting where social and cultural experimentation could replace the old order of things that had presumably proven unworkable.

In this the Japanese were particularly sensitive to the apparent failure of liberalism, capitalism, and other tenets of Western civilization whose hegemony had been taken for granted. Japan's scholars, journalists, and politicians were quick to grasp the fact that Europeans and Americans were seriously questioning, many of them going so far as to abandon as no longer valid, age-old doctrines of democratic government, free competition, private enterprise, and the like. All this was caused by the deepening economic crisis, but the search for a solution to the crisis became less and less limited to economic policy and took on more and more cultural connotations. This was because, in facing what many believed to be the unprecedented economic disaster of the modern world, it was inevitable that such questions as the relationship between citizen and state, social justice, and even human nature had to be faced. Not surprisingly, more and more spoke of the malaise of Western civilization and of the need to attempt a fundamental restructuring of society.

Such attempts in themselves were nothing new. Even during the heyday of capitalism and liberal democracy during the 1920s, socialists had continued to advocate state ownership of the means of production. They had been joined by fascists, who argued that free enterprise was incompatible with the well-being of the state and that only a corporatist structure would work to integrate individuals into the state. In the early 1930s these viewpoints came to be taken seriously, even in hitherto unrestricted capitalist economies and self-assured democracies such as Britain and the United States, where officials and opinion leaders were willing to experiment with greater governmental initiatives in the production and distribution of goods and services. Classical liberalism, which had already been supplemented, if not displaced, by some sort of corporatism even in capital-ist countries, was openly attacked as deficient, and many questioned the validity of party politics or parliamentary democracy in an age of economic turmoil.

What the Japanese occupiers of Manchuria were trying to do could be best understood as part of this global trend, the search for a new basis of national organization after the liberal formula for political and economic affairs had appar-ently become bankrupt. That may have been why the archi-tects of Manchurian economic planning never tired of stressing the moral basis of the new experiment.[18] The idea was to put an end to private initiatives that presumably had led to the ruin of capitalism and to substitute a controlled economy under the supervision of the state. Such ideas had the support not only of the army and right-wing nationalists but also of an increasing number of Japanese socialists and even liberals—or, one should say, those who used to be socialists and liberals but who now were willing to accept the idea of state control. We could of course argue that in Japan, in contrast to the West, the legacy of liberalism and capitalism had been much weaker to begin with, and there-fore that the adoption of a near totalitarian order of things in Manchuria must not have required as drastic a reorienta-tion as in some other countries. True enough, but to ignore the transition in Japanese thinking would be to belittle the achievements of liberalism and capitalism that had taken place during the 1920s and to make no distinction between the two decades. That would be untenable.

What seems to have happened was that those in Japan who once had stood for a peaceful definition of foreign affairs and for the primacy of economics and culture over military power now accepted the military conquest of Man-churia in the belief that the Manchurian experiment could lead to the establishment of a haven, an alternative to the capitalist ways that had been discredited not only in Japan but all over the world.

An interesting development in this connection was the fact that a sizable number of Japanese went to Manchuria to engage in educational and cultural activities. In the late 1930s there were over 6,300 primary schools in the region, teaching more than one million children between the ages of six and ten. At the apex of the educational pyramid was the new Kenkoku Daigaku, or Hsinching (Shinkyō) University, aimed at producing "pioneering leaders in the establishment of a moral world," as a propaganda leaflet explained. Here and elsewhere the Japanese in Manchuria talked of creating a new culture, different from Western liberalism and designed for "the awakening of Asia." This popular expression, which went back to the pan-Asianists of the late nineteenth century, now took on much more specific meaning because of the crisis of Western capitalism and democracy. Manchuria was to be an Asian alternative to the bankrupt Western way of life. If it worked there, then it could become the basis for similar experimentation elsewhere in Asia. It is not surprising under the circumstances that throughout occupied Manchuria the Japanese should have built movie studios, disseminated newspapers, and organized cultural associations to spread the word. [19] Young Japanese residents in the conquered territory—the Kwantung army was trying to settle hundreds of thousands of them in frontier areas as farmer-soldiers—were systematically indoctrinated in the idea of mission, to view the region as their new homeland where all peoples lived in harmony. A series of children's books published in the late 1930s sought to acquaint the reader with Manchuria's history, geography, and customs and included short stories with themes stressing Chinese-Manchurian-Japanese cooperation and understanding in building a new society.[20]

Clearly these were self-serving endeavors, and there is no reason to believe that non-Japanese children and adults in Manchuria were persuaded by such propaganda. But in the Three Eastern Provinces at least talk of building a new society may have made some sense, given the region's historical distance from the rest of China as well as its relative isolation from the politics and culture of China proper. The situation was vastly different south of the Great Wall. Here too, however, the Japanese were eager to couple military action with a cultural offensive. One of their main designs was to establish "new people's associations" (*hsin-min hui*) in occupied areas to serve as centers for indoctrinating local populations. With their headquarters in Nanking, these organizations in various parts of North China conducted classes, held fairs, and promoted other kinds of cultural activities in which both Chinese and Japanese participated. The total number of Chinese involved in such activities was very small, perhaps not even 1 percent of the population under Japanese control, but Japanese civilians took the project seriously, bringing teachers and community organizers from the homeland for the purpose. The very title of the organization—"new people" or "people's renovation"—expressed the by then favorite theme of the war: to revitalize and rejuvenate China so as to bring the two countries closer together in their joint mission of renovating the whole of Asia.[21]

At home Japan's intellectual as well as military and governmental leaders echoed the same idea, that through the war in China Japan was trying to establish a new moral order. Yasuoka Masahiro, a leading nationalist ideologue, asserted that Japan was "the most sacred existence on earth with its moral ideals." This he pitted against the liberal and communist conceptions of state in the West. Endowing the state with a personality and with moral principles was something that was also happening in fascist and Nazi thought in Europe, but Yasuoka sought to distance Japan from Italy or Germany by arguing that Asia had been enslaved by the white nations and denied freedom and personality. The goal of Japan's "sacred war" was to purge Asia of the dominating influence of the West, which had manifested itself in modern civilization with its stress on greedy competition and on inanimate machinery. Japan, and Asia, in contrast, would be characterized by collective harmony and by the human spirit.[22]

Such ideas were repeated with monotonous regularity after 1938, when the Chinese war entered its second, prolonged phase as the Tokyo government abandoned all attempts at a negotiated settlement with the Nationalist regime. By then of course the rape of Nanking and other instances of indiscriminate slaughtering of Chinese civilians had taken place, exposing the hypocrisy of talk of a new moral task. The butchering of innocent people belied any pretense at building a new culture. Or perhaps the massacres were a product of the new culture in the sense that it assumed Japanese superiority and leadership. It may well have been that, given the increasingly stringent wartime censorship and the built-in biases of war-reporting, most Japanese were unaware of the magnitude of the Nanking and other tragedies and went on thinking that the war was taking place between the righteous Japanese and the recalcitrant Chinese. By giving the term "culture" an anthropological meaning, it could even be said that the massacring of Chinese civilians was a cultural phenomenon, reflecting a culture of brutalization, of perversity, of wanton violence, a culture that completely ignored international law or any distinction between combatant and civilization, between war and peace.

Just as the contemporaneous Nazi murders of Jews and other minorities were derived from a certain cultural attitude, Japanese atrocities revealed how deficient in basic decency millions were becoming at that time. To say that other countries were also becoming brutalized—William Shirer recorded in his diary in 1939 that the world of the 1920s ("free, civilized, deepening, full of minor tragedy and joy and work and leisure, new lands, new faces") had been replaced by "darkness. A new world. Blackout, bombs, slaughter, Nazism . . . the night and the shrieks and barbarism"—does not mean that Nazi behavior and Japanese behavior were interchangeable phenomena, nor does it excuse Japanese barbarism by viewing it as an aspect of global barbarism. But we must remind ourselves that brutalization was not simply a byproduct of a war; it existed under the Nazi regime long before war came. Rather it may be argued that in Japan, as in Germany or Italy, the atmosphere of what Fritz Stern calls "cultural despair" was removing self-restraint, self-discipline, a sense of compassion from interpersonal relations.[23] In the Japanese case there may have been nothing comparable to Nazi attacks on the minorities at home, but the same lack of compassion was clearly evident once Japanese soldiers and civilians went to China.

In such an atmosphere, and despite what was reported about the Nanking and other incidents, it is all the more remarkable that so many Japanese writers, official and non-official, should have continued to state ardently their belief that Japan did not desire to crush or conquer China, that the two countries must cooperate for their common good, and that there was some historical and moral significance to this task. By endowing the frustrating war with historical meaning, the propagandists were in effect saying that the fighting in China was more a cultural than a conventional military enterprise. It is striking how often the word "culture" appears in their writings. Ozaki Hotsumi talked of "the cultural stage" at which Japan allegedly had arrived; this, he said, was what defined the nature of the Chinese war. Sugihara Masami, who apparently coined the phrase "Tōa kyōdōtai" (East Asian cooperative order), wrote that Japan aimed at promoting a new cultural consciousness in Asia, a consciousness opposed to Western cultural consciousness and one that was to create a new worldview. That worldview would reject both capitalism and communism and would awaken and unify Asia under alternative principles. Rōyama Masamichi agreed, noting that this new awareness should enable the Asians to make use of their respective cultures in such a way as to oppose Western civilization and pave the way for a world culture. The Chinese-Japanese war, wrote Matsumoto Gaku, was taking place at a critical turning point in history, when individualism and class-consciousness were giving way to a new vision of world culture, one placing less emphasis on politics and economics and more on cultural communication. Intellectuals and "cultural people" (*bunkajin*) in all countries should cooperate in this task, with those in Japan playing the leading role.[24]

Saying that these were self-serving statements does not help us understand why the Japanese at that time were so anxious to put a cultural construction on the Chinese war. The concept of culture seemingly functioned as a way, perhaps the only way, to explain the untenable war on the continent. Since it could not be justified on the usual strategic or economic grounds, culture provided a plausible alternative. To call the war a cultural undertaking enabled the Japanese to assert that this was unlike other, more aggressive wars. Fujisawa Chikao, the ideologue of the Hsin-min movement in north China, argued that Japan might have to use force and temporarily occupy China, but that these were means for a nobler end, to usher in an age of "new cultural principles." These principles, he added, would be the basis of a totalitarian culture that was certain to replace the "false culture of liberalism."[25] Here we can see that the term "culture" served Japan's domestic needs, justifying the suppression of traditional cultural pursuits so that they would give way to a totalitarian environment uniting part and whole, individual and nation. By focusing on the theme of culture it was easy to theorize about the partnership with Germany and Italy, for their totalitarian regimes too could be described as a cultural experiment, an alternative to the defunct bourgeois or communist variety. For all these reasons Japanese writings in the late 1930s became saturated with cultural themes.

Perhaps the ultimate statements in this category were made by the editors of the Kokusai Bunka Shinkōkai (KBS), the Japan Society for International Cultural Relations, which was established in 1934. That was the same year the British Council had been founded, a coincidence indicating that there was some shared awareness of the need to engage in cultural offensives and promote cross-cultural affairs as part of a nation's foreign policy. Until 1940 *Kokusai bunka* (International Culture), the journal of the KBS, maintained a low profile, stressing the importance of cultural understanding and cooperation with other countries, including the United States and Europe. The organization arranged study groups and held symposia, concerning China in particular, in order to devise better methods for pursuing an

effective cultural policy in wartime. At one of the work-
shops on cultural relations with China a Foreign Ministry
spokesman stated that the Japanese must persuade the Chinese that they had a stake in amalgamating traditional Asian
and modern Western civilizations so as to create a new
world culture. The task, another participant asserted, was
fundamentally a cultural one and could never be settled by
war. KBS leaders reiterated these themes time and again, a
rather innocuous exercise. But starting in 1940, *Kokusai
bunka* editorials began to support the war effort much more
explicitly and called for subordinating cultural policy to that
effort. The new order in Asia, a lead essay asserted, must
first be established by force and then reinforced by economic and cultural underpinnings. Even so, the vocabulary
was the same. This essay spoke of the goal of Asian liberation, the need to awaken the Asians to their own cultural
ideals.[26] Because the KBS had long been identified with
what remained of Japan's internationalism, it was a serious
development to reject it so easily in favor of a self-centered
conception of Asian culture. The reasoning was no different
from that of many others who, like the legal scholar Tamura
Tokuji, asserted that Japan was pursuing a "new internationalism," different from the old internationalism of the
status-quo-oriented nations. Instead, Japan was aiming at
a world order that went beyond traditional definitions of
interstate relations and united several countries sharing "a
new Asian culture."[27]

Examples could be multiplied indefinitely. They would be
of far less interest but for the fact that the obsession with
cultural vocabulary was not confined to Japan. In their resistance to Japanese aggression the Chinese too spoke of culture, in a sense responding in kind to Japan's cultural render-

ing of the war. As early as March 1932 Ts'ai Yüan-p'ei, the noted philosopher and president of the Academia Sinica, was appealing to the League of Nations to condemn the Japanese army's "wholesale destruction of China's educational and cultural establishments" as it engaged in its aggressive war in Manchuria and elsewhere in China. "Wherever the arms of Japanese militarism reach," he said, "China's educational and cultural organs collapse under their wanton aerial and artillery bombardment."[28] Here was clear recognition that the military struggle involved a cultural conflict, and that for the Chinese to defend their sovereignty meant first and foremost the preservation of their cultural institutions.

China's anti-Japanese struggle was aimed not only at defeating Japanese ambitions but also at transforming Chinese society and culture. Chinese intellectuals and students were among the first to organize a nationwide movement to resist Japan. It has been called the December Ninth movement to commemorate the massive demonstrations held in Peking on that day in 1935 protesting the establishment of a Japanese-controlled separate government in north China. By then the Comintern thesis about creating a popular front of all anti-fascist forces had been promulgated, so the anti-Japanese movement could embrace all factions and forces in China. The movement was profoundly cultural in that the student and intellectual leaders recognized the need for mobilizing the masses in order to awake in them the spirit of national salvation and domestic transformation. These were themes from the May Fourth movement, and in fact the popular-front strategy had much in common with it; both were nationwide campaigns committed to cultural renewal and change.

What kind of change? This was a particularly important

question in the 1930s because Japanese propaganda was stressing the war's cultural dimension. The Chinese would have to respond to the Japanese contention that Western civilization was in decline, as well as to the Japanese invitation for constructing a pan-Asian cultural order. Some, like Hu Shih, staunchly reiterated the May Fourth theme of Westernization, arguing that Japan had never really been as Westernized as it appeared on the surface. Now that Japan was turning its back, China had an opportunity to champion Western values, to become their defender in Asia.

But that seems to have been a minority view, at least at the outset. Chinese intellectuals too were affected by the universal sense of disillusionment with modern Western civilization that pervaded the world in the early years of the Depression. In that atmosphere some turned to the kind of fascism Chiang Kai-shek advocated, but many more embraced radical ideologies. To them the Soviet Union rather than Nazi Germany represented the wave of the future, and Marxist ideology made it much easier than Nazism to account for China's plight. Both groups could agree on the fundamental ideology of national salvation, but the leaders of the December Ninth movement viewed anti-Japanese resistance as part of a worldwide process of social and cultural transformation. Various proclamations by students and intellectuals in the wake of the December 9 demonstration called on the nation to unite to regain lost territory; at the same time they urged the government to guarantee freedom of the press, assembly, and publication. On December 10 students at Peking University declared that the China problem was part of a larger global question: the old world order was obviously crumbling, so China must side with the forces that were struggling for liberation from past bondages. "We must cooperate and struggle alongside all the oppressed peoples of the world and with the countries that treat our nation in a spirit of equality."[29] The students would coordinate their action with their counterparts in other parts of China and struggle for domestic freedom as well as liberation from imperialism. They would oppose the existing system of education, which, they said, enslaved the nation; they would mobilize the masses as they freely expressed their will to change the status quo.

Such utterances were not limited to radical students. After the formation of the second united front in 1937, the Nationalists incorporated the same vocabulary into their war effort against Japan. Chiang Kai-shek declared that the war with Japan pitted China's Three People's Principles against Japanese imperialism, China's superior spirit to Japan's military might, and Chinese culture against Japanese barbarism. The Chinese Communists could not have agreed more. They put renewed emphasis on the Three People's Principles in their anti-Japanese campaign, for, they asserted, these principles were the guide to national salvation and reconstruction that must ultimately be built on wholesale cultural transformation. It would require uniting all the occupational and professional groups in China, unifying them so as to mobilize the masses. Externally it would be crucial to engage in an ideological offensive by sending educational and other leaders abroad to spread the word about Japanese brutality and the Chinese determination to resist. As the Communist party declared in 1938, China must try to influence Western books, newspapers, and movies.[30]

Such efforts led to an emphasis on democracy, the belief that China's struggle was part of the global movement for the survival of democracy. In 1936 the Communists had defined the country as a democratic republic; now the renewed acceptance of the Three People's Principles confirmed it. Not only had most of the ideas Mao Tse-tung presented in his pivotal 1940 essay, "On the People's Democracy," been anticipated by statements he and his comrades had made since 1936, the Nationalists also had expressed similar thoughts. The declaration of the Kuomintang's emergency people's congress held in April 1938 asserted that the party aimed not only at expelling the foreign invaders but also at reconstructing the nation on the basis of freedom and equality. This dual task, the congress declared, must be carried on simultaneously, and both depended on the people's ability to organize themselves and develop a capacity for self-defense and self-government. All Chinese must rededicate themselves to this revolution, and their leaders must realize that ultimately the country's salvation lay in a new cultural movement that applied the insights of the natural and social sciences to national life. Given such a perspective, it was not surprising that several Communist leaders, including Mao, should have participated in a new national political assembly organized by the government in 1938. This 200-member organization held its first conference in July that year and condemned Japan's brutal treatment of innocent Chinese, declaring that Japan was intent not only upon destroying China's independence but also obliterating its culture.[31]

All such expressions of cultural nationalism and of a commitment to universal values indicate how difficult it must have been for Japanese propagandists to persuade the Chinese to embrace their brand of pan-Asian cultural renewal against Western civilization. Chinese statements of the period, coming from all political persuasions, constantly reiterated the theme that China's struggle had the support of "world public opinion" and was part of the global quest for peace and justice. The fact that such ideas had become commonplace in China by the late 1930s is significant, for they anticipated by one or two years what would emerge in the West as the dominant ideology of the Second World War. By the time Franklin D. Roosevelt and Winston Churchill met in August 1941 at Argentia Bay and issued the Atlantic Charter, the Chinese had clearly defined their struggle as one of democracy against totalitarianism and aggression, reiterating the theme of the May Fourth movement, now strengthened through the crucible of war. Japan was to find itself more isolated than ever, not just strategically but ideologically as well.

Japan had lost the war even before it was defeated in the battlefield. It failed to succeed as well as China in the search for a new cultural order, a task confronting all countries in the 1930s. The Japanese took the task seriously but ended up going to war in the name of culture, whereas the Chinese, as Chiang Kai-shek said in 1939, could hold their own because they had confidence in their glorious tradition which was being reinforced by certain universally shared civilizational values.[32] Earlier, around the turn of the century, Japan did better than China because of its single-minded dedication to military power in a world environment that gave primacy to the power factor. During the 1920s and the 1930s, however, when issues of cultural association, survival, and redefinition grew in importance throughout the world, China was much more successful. That need not have been. If economics, the third factor besides power and culture, had been allowed to remain a major determinant of international affairs after 1929, the cultural liaison between China and Japan might have taken a different form. It remained to be seen how, after the Second World War, when economics returned to center stage in international affairs, the two countries would redefine their relationship.

III

Economics

Nothing is more striking in the postwar history of Chinese-Japanese relations than the primacy of economics. From the resumption of trade between the two countries in the immediate aftermath of the war to the recent massive infusion of Japanese capital and technology to help assist China's modernization efforts, economic ties have steadily expanded, until today they constitute one of the most solid links in world affairs. This scale of bilateral economic interdependence is unprecedented in the history of the two countries. At the end of the nineteenth century and the beginning of the twentieth Chinese-Japanese relations were defined fundamentally by military power, whereas during the interwar years cultural forces became significant. Economic ties had always existed, but before the First World War they tended to be subordinate to the military equation, and in the 1930s they were but part of a struggle between two opposing conceptions of Asian order. During the 1920s economics did play an important, even decisive, role, but it became submerged under revolutionary upheavals of an ideological nature after the onset of the global Depression. It was only after Japan's defeat that economics reasserted its central role in defining the bilateral relationship.

Was this, like earlier periods of history, a reflection of worldwide trends? What had happened to the power and cultural dimensions? Even if economics has been the key to postwar Chinese-Japanese relations, can we expect this to continue in the years ahead? These are intriguing and complicated questions to which I can offer only tentative answers. For the sake of clarity I shall subdivide the postwar years into five segments: the immediate aftermath of the war (1945–1949); from 1949 to the late 1950s; from the late 1950s to the late 1960s; from the late 1960s to the early 1980s; and recent years.

In the immediate wake of the war military power as such disappeared as an issue insofar as Japan was concerned, although the Chinese continued to worry about the potential resurgence of Japanese militarism. But clearly, in the aftermath of defeat, Japan would never again be in a position to exercise power unilaterally. It would be disarmed, its troops repatriated, its overseas bases dismantled, and its colonies taken away. China, in contrast, was to have emerged as one of the major powers, the key factor on which the peace and stability of Asia would depend.

In reality China was unable to assume that role because of internal strife, which was dividing its military force into two camps, one tied closely to the Soviet Union and the other to the United States. The Chinese were aware that the renewed civil war made it difficult, if not impossible, for the nation to function as a military power. Less than a year after Japan's defeat, commentators in China were noting the ironic contrast between their internal strife and the situation in Japan which, as one of them wrote, "despite its crushing defeat, resulting from our eight years' struggle, is already raising its head again, thanks to America's positive assistance." On July 7, 1946, the Chinese Communist party declared that the remnants of Japanese fascism and American reactionaries were assisting China's reactionary forces to steal the fruits of victory from the Chinese people. These and other statements revealed the deep misgivings among Chinese of all camps right after the war that Japanese militarism might rise again, that all the sacrifices of the long war for national salvation might prove to have been in vain.[1] Still, even the most alarmist observers in China recognized that Japanese military power would not be able to challenge China again without the assistance of the United States. In other words, Chinese-Japanese power relations were now becoming part of the global power system in which the United States and the Soviet Union enjoyed hegemonic positions. Given such circumstances, neither China nor Japan would enjoy military autonomy. Accordingly, economic and cultural factors would be of greater significance in the initial postwar phase of Chinese-Japanese relations.

Not surprisingly, economic considerations weighed heavily with the Japanese government. Although its authority was severely restricted by the Occupation authorities, Tokyo's officials from early on were convinced that the most urgent issues facing the defeated nation were economic: how to feed, house, and clothe the population whose number was increasing daily as war veterans streamed back to the homeland from the Asian continent and the Pacific islands. For Japanese officials—and here we should note that, as a result of the purge of some 200,000 leaders from government, business, and educational positions of influence, a younger generation was replacing them—it was obvious that economic recovery hinged on foreign trade and that the most accessible markets would still have to be found on the Asian continent. With much of its heavy industry destroyed or dismantled, the best the Japanese could hope for would be to provide China with textiles, dinnerware, and such items as had penetrated the Asian markets prior to the 1930s. They would be an important means for securing foreign exchange with which to pay for much needed raw materials and foodstuffs.

The reasoning was virtually interchangeable with that in the early Meiji years, but this time the country was under a foreign occupation with a mandate to remake it as a peaceful nation, distinct from the power model of the Meiji state. Fortunately for Japan, trade was not totally forbidden, even in the immediate postwar period. The Occupation authorities recognized the need to allow Japan limited trade and shipping, which was necessary not only to feed the people but also to enable the country to produce surplus earnings which could be transferred to other Asian countries as war reparations. Interestingly, by 1946 Japanese exports amounted to over 2 billion yen, about the same value as the export trade recorded in 1934. Meanwhile commodity prices had increased more than ten times, and the value of the yen vis-à-vis the dollar had been cut drastically (a dollar being worth 2 yen in 1934 but something like 270 yen by 1946–1947), so it is meaningless to compare such figures. Even so, what stands out is the consistent growth of Japanese trade after the war. Its exports increased from 2 billion yen in 1946 to 170 billion in 1949. This latter figure, the equivalent of about 510 million dollars, was more or less the same as that in 1941, a remarkable pace of recovery for a war-devastated nation. Even such rapid expansion, however, barely kept up with the growth of imports, and chronic trade imbalances existed. All the more reason, then, to expand the nearby markets.

In 1946 about two-thirds of Japanese exports went to the United States and the rest to Asia, but in 1949 close to 50 percent of exports were for Asia, more than double the amount going to America. Because Japan was always running up trade deficits with regard to the United States, whereas it was selling more to Asian countries than buying from them, the zeal with which the Japanese sought to expand their trade with China is understandable. Throughout 1946 Japanese exports to China far exceeded imports, prompting many Chinese to urge that the situation be rectified by expanding their own export trade, particularly in Southeast Asia now that this region had been evacuated by Japanese troops. Equally important, Chinese observers insisted that whatever the Japanese gained in their trade should be earmarked for reparations payments to help China industrialize. *Takung pao* urged in October 1946 that the nation quickly end its civil war, obtain sufficient reparations from Japan, and use them for industrial reconstruction. Otherwise, Japan would continue to be more advanced economically than China and remain "the greatest power in East Asia."[2] (Although Chiang Kai-shek had declared in the wake of Japan's defeat that China would not demand war reparations, Chinese commentators ignored his statement and assumed that Japanese reparations would play a role in postwar economic reconstruction.)

Unfortunately the civil war in China did not abate. It not only slowed Chinese recovery but also checked the growth of the bilateral trade, with the result that until the mid-1950s India and Pakistan purchased more from Japan than China did.

The perceived importance of the economic liaison between the two countries right after the war is clear, but how about the cultural dimension? Here the post-1945 years marked an abrupt shift from the 1930s, when Japan's cultural offensive as well as cultural malaise had been met by China's reaffirmation of its own and of Western cultural values. Now Japan's pan-Asianist ideology had been thoroughly discredited, and a wholesale Americanization of Japanese culture began, ranging from educational reform to the reintroduction of American movies and sports. Postwar

Japan went through a period of self-mortification. Reaction against, or revulsion about, wartime propaganda produced a loss of confidence and intellectual uncertainty. The spiritual vacuum was filled mostly by American-inspired and American-imposed ideas and artifacts. Under such circumstances Japan had little or nothing to offer culturally in redefining Chinese-Japanese relations.

At the same time, it is not difficult to detect a secondary theme of Chinese-Japanese cultural rapprochement at this time. Within a year after August 1945, as many as 180 articles on China were published in Japanese periodicals. This indicated a genuine interest in maintaining intellectual ties between the two countries and, more important, a widespread sense that the Japanese had been totally misinformed about China and that they must do everything possible to rectify the situation. In 1946 a group of radical and reform-minded Japanese organized a China study institute (Chūgoku Kenkyūjo), convinced that "for the future of a democratic Japan, the scientific study of contemporary China is an absolute imperative." The association began publishing mimeographed sheets of articles about China, some of which were translations from Chinese writings. Another publication, Chūgoku shiryō (Materials on China), was launched in November 1946; its initial issue asserted that "to know China is to know the world. It is also to know the future of Japan." Kuo Mo-jo contributed a message, saying the Chinese and the Japanese had much to learn from one another and that only through a deepened cultural exchange could they hope to surmount the obstacles in the way of their understanding.[3]

It is not surprising that the Japanese, repentant of their aggressive war, should have been particularly sensitive to Chinese views on the war as well as on postwar Japanese developments. Journals were filled with excerpts from Chinese writings on Japanese democratization, land reform, political change, and other phenomena. From these accounts it appears that the Chinese were especially sensitive on the emperor question. The indignities and atrocities they had suffered had been carried out by Japanese troops in the name of the emperor, and in the immediate postwar years Chinese opinion strongly favored abolishing the imperial institution or at least retaining it only as a harmless symbol. Many Chinese expressed dissatisfaction with the new Japanese constitution, drafted under American Occupation auspices in 1946; they contended that it had not done enough to emasculate the emperor system. "In order to prevent the resurgence of Japanese aggression," asserted *Shen pao*, a moderate daily, "the first priority is to eliminate the emperor institution and state Shintō." T'ien Han, the playwright encountered in Chapter II, was quoted as saying that he hoped the Japanese writers and people would take immediate steps to rid themselves of the emperor ideology. Both Kuomintang and Communist organs of opinion insisted that the new Japanese constitution retained the influence of reactionaries surrounding the throne. As long as this group remained protected, there was a chance that Japan would rearm and engage in another aggressive war.[4]

By reprinting such essays Japanese editors were seeking to atone for the war guilt. One wrote that in order to do so, it was imperative to follow developments in China closely and to consider ways in which the two countries could cooperate in the interest of peace.[5] It would be interesting to examine how widespread such a perspective was, and how influenced postwar Japanese opinion was by currents of thought in China. Despite its vital importance, this subject does not seem to have received scholarly attention.

Nor have the ways in which the Chinese input into postwar Japanese thought competed with American influence been studied. It may well be that, but for the civil war, the competition might have been keener, for it seems possible that in the immediate postwar years the Japanese were open to and sensitive about both Chinese and American viewpoints and interested in listening to their respective castigations of Japan's war crimes.

Although in time, because of the Chinese civil war as well as the onset of the Cold War, Chinese influence abated and American influence became predominant in Japan, we can detect a theme in postwar Japanese intellectual history that resisted wholesale Americanization and sought to retain China's role as the major framework for cultural discourse. In a famous essay published in 1948, Takeuchi Yoshimi argued that it was wrong to view Japan in the Western framework and compare the country to China only with the yardstick of modern capitalist civilization. In such a framework Japan might seem more modernized than China, but in fact, he wrote, Japan's pseudo-Westernization or superficial modernization had been no match for China's much more solid civilization, which was more advanced than that of Japan precisely because it had rejected superficial Westernization.[6] Such views appealed to those in Japan who sought to make their country's wartime aggression toward China the point of departure for postwar Japanese society and culture, to make China the basis for constructing a new society and ideology.

These ideas could have gained greater influence in Japan, particularly among those who felt uneasy about accepting the American definition of world affairs—the Cold War—as the sole framework in which to consider national and international affairs. The Cold War framework would force the Japanese to view developments in China and elsewhere

in Asia in terms of the struggle between the forces of freedom (or capitalism) and communism. But given the "re-
verse course" in Japan after 1947–48, when radical movements were steadily replaced by the "old liberalism"
represented by Prime Minister Yoshida Shigeru, it became
more and more difficult to advocate close ties to China as
the key to Japan's future. And as the deepening civil war in
China made it increasingly difficult for Chinese and Japanese to maintain contact, this phase of Chinese-Japanese
cultural relations proved much less productive than their
advocates had hoped.

Nevertheless, the term "culture" remained a key concept
through which Chinese and Japanese associated with one
another after the war. Although, as noted earlier, in Japan
the term had been little more than a wartime propaganda
device to cover up aggressive behavior, somehow it retained
its centrality in the Japanese imagination. The nation, the
minister of education asserted within days after Japan's sur-
render, must be reborn as one dedicated to cultural pursuits.
Culture was contrasted to military power; the pursuit of
culture was now considered the only alternative to aggressive war. Japan, wrote Hoashi Riichirō, a noted philosopher, in 1949, had decided to transform itself from a militaristic to a cultural nation.[7]

But was there any guarantee that the postwar Japanese
"culture" might not prove to be yet another euphemism
for aggression? According to Hoashi, the solution lay in
combining the merits of Eastern and Western cultures in
order to develop a new world civilization. This sounded
little different from the official rhetoric of the 1930s, reveal-
ing how difficult it was to go beyond trite formulations in
a discourse on culture. But Hoashi was convinced that the
amalgamation of East and West was possible through peaceful means, whereas in the 1930s the same idea was used to

justify the Chinese war. This was all the more reason to befriend the Chinese and to try to learn from them. If the two peoples could cooperate culturally, it would contribute not only to establishing Japan as a cultural nation but also to developing a new global civilization.

In China too there was considerable interest in the idea of an Asian cultural mission. In 1948 a new journal, *Ya-chou shih-chih* (Asian Century), was started in Shanghai, with a view to promoting "world peace and prosperity" and to "creating a world culture." In order to carry out such objectives, the editors noted, there was much that the Japanese could do, now that they had recognized the error of utilizing Western civilization for aggressive ends in Asia. They, the Chinese, and other Asians must now join forces to liberate Asia and usher in a new Asian century.[8]

Unfortunately for the development of such postwar visions of Asian culture, the Chinese and Japanese soon were to reduce, if not to sever entirely, their intellectual ties. Many of the Japanese radicals who might have wished to retain the momentum began looking toward the Soviet Union, while others rediscovered American and European pacifism and internationalism. Chinese intellectuals, engulfed in a civil war, paid less and less attention to joint cultural pursuits with their Japanese counterparts. Nevertheless, the legacies of the immediate postwar years, now almost forgotten, are worth recalling if only because they provide a point of continuity between prewar and postwar Chinese-Japanese cultural relations.

These features of Chinese-Japanese relations during 1945–1949—power's decreased role, the renewed importance of trade, and cultural connections where there were some genuine, although often contradictory and frustrating, efforts at reconciliation—would continue to characterize the bilateral relationship after 1949, the year of the Communist victory in China. At the power level the picture would have to be modified considerably of course, because during the years from 1949 through the 1950s China emerged as a unified military power and Japan undertook a modest rearmament. Military power again became a factor, but the key question would be how such developments were related to other aspects of the bilateral relationship.

Too often the story has been put in the framework of the Cold War. The American-Soviet confrontation that had begun in such countries as Poland, Germany, Iran, Greece, and Turkey became steadily globalized, and by 1949–50 most of the world was divided into two power blocs. Both China and Japan played a role in this development. To be more exact, they were incorporated into the bipolar international system. China and the Soviet Union entered into a military alliance at the beginning of 1950; a year and a half later Japan concluded a security pact with the United States. In 1950 and 1951 American and Chinese forces clashed in Korea, and the peninsula became divided—one part tied to the Soviet-Chinese camp and the other to the American-Japanese camp. Henceforth regional stability would hinge on some balance between these two sides, and there would be little contact between them. The Cold War had unmistakably come to Asia.

Because China and Japan belonged to two hostile camps in a divided world, by definition they were potential enemies. And that of course had a power aspect. As soon as the Korean war broke out, in June 1950, Japan began its rearmament program with the encouragement of the Occupation authorities. The core of the new army and navy consisted of Imperial army and navy officers now "depurged" for the purpose. Japanese minesweepers were sent to the Korean coasts to assist the American war effort. It is not surprising that the Chinese, given their misgivings about the revival of Japanese militarism, should have reacted with alarm. Undoubtedly, this was a factor behind Peking's decision to send "volunteer" forces across the Yalu in the fall of 1950 to prevent American forces from unifying the whole of Korea, thereby assisting, the Chinese contended, the return of Japanese militarism to the continent.

In the meantime, as the United States government took steps to prevent Taiwan's unification with mainland China, Japan became tied to the former. China was not represented at the San Francisco peace conference held in September 1951 because neither Peking nor Taipei would give up its claim to speak for the whole country. The United States, however, pressed Japan to conclude a separate peace treaty with Taipei. It is noteworthy that Prime Minister Yoshida, in agreeing to the step, justified the action by arguing that the Chinese-Soviet treaty of alliance was a military arrangement directed against Japan, and that Japan could not be expected to enter into treaty relations with a regime that had so clearly identified itself with the anti-American side in the bipolar world. The Chinese, for their part, denounced the Yoshida policy as evidence that the United States and Japan were preparing an aggressive war against China. America, Japan, and Taiwan were accused of plotting another imperialistic war in Asia. Under the circumstances, Peking declared, China would refuse to recognize the validity of Japan's peace treaty with the Nationalist government on Taiwan and would consider that a state of war remained between the two countries.[9]

After the Korean war Asia became even more rigidly

divided by a series of mutual-security pacts the United States signed with countries surrounding China, while the Chinese undertook to modernize their armed forces to solidify its position in the power system. Meanwhile the Japanese, after gaining sovereignty in 1952, retained and increased their armed forces. True, compared with the prewar years, Japan's arms spending was much more modest; the share of military expenditures in annual governmental outlays was only around 10 percent, about one-half to one-third of the pre-1941 figures. Moreover, although defense spending increased by 50 percent between 1952 and 1960, governmental expenditures more than doubled, so the ratio between the two continued to decline. But Japan's limited armament was amply supplemented by American military power, so the Chinese might well have felt the situation was, if anything, even more ominous than before the Second World War, when they could count on the United States to check Japan's armed force. The militarization of the Cold War, a key phenomenon of international affairs during the 1950s, clearly affected Chinese-Japanese relations.

But that was not the whole story. As it had during the immediate postwar period, the economic aspect of Chinese-Japanese relations evolved with its own momentum, only slightly affected by the Cold War. In June 1952, as soon as the San Francisco peace treaty went into effect, Japanese businessmen negotiated a trade agreement with Chinese authorities. It was not a governmental agreement since, technically speaking, in view of the Japanese peace treaty with Taipei, there was no official relationship between Tokyo and Peking. Nevertheless, the Japanese government encouraged such commercial links with mainland China, fully cognizant of the importance of the continental market for Japanese trade. Although Japanese export to the People's Republic was circumscribed by the so-called Chincom and Cocom restrictions, which forbade the sale of strategically sensitive items to China and other Communist countries, that did not prevent the resumption and steady growth of trade. Both Japanese businessmen and Chinese officials were eager to conduct bilateral trade outside the power framework. China could use Japanese textiles, bicycles, sewing machines, and other commodities; it could offer Japan, soybeans, coal, and other raw materials. Already in 1951 the trade amounted to about $200 million, or 6 percent of Japan's total trade and 10 percent of China's. It is true that initially much of the trade took the form of barter arrangements—exchanging China's coal for Japanese textile machinery, for instance. All the same, even the conservative Japanese leadership recognized the potential importance of the China market and did not stand in the way of the private business missions that were dispatched to the mainland as early as spring 1952. From then until the late 1950s the bilateral trade recorded steady growth, although it was not until somewhat later, in the 1960s, that Japan's trade with the China mainland came to exceed that with Taiwan.

Postwar Chinese-Japanese trade, however, never regained the relative importance it had before the war, and the degree of economic interdependence between the two countries was less pronounced. In postwar Japanese recovery, for instance, in terms of real per-capita income the level attained in the mid-1930s was reached again in 1953; but this resulted less from the return to the China market than from the Korean war. That war created unanticipated demand for Japanese supplies and equipment for the United States armed forces, totaling some 492 million dollars. Since

Japan's GNP was then only about 10 billion dollars, this windfall did much to launch the economy on its way to speedy recovery. In that sense Japan owed its postwar economic development to a war in which it was not a direct participant but in which China had to divert scarce resources to fight American forces equipped with Japanese material. Japan benefited even as China suffered from the Korean war.

Following the Korean war, moreover, Japan could afford to spend proportionally more of its resources on economic development than China could, particularly industrialization to expand export trade. Although Japan remained a net importer throughout the 1950s—it was only in 1965 that it began to record favorable balances of trade—its total volume grew threefold between 1950 and 1956. Thus the United States government felt justified in sponsoring Japan's membership in the General Agreement on Tariffs and Trade, a sort of a coming-out party for the country as a trading nation. To that extent, Japanese recovery, industrialization, and trade expansion developed in the context of the Cold War and were assisted much more through close ties with the United States than with China.

China had to do without American help and with relatively little Japanese economic input as it sought to put an end to the economic chaos brought about by the Japanese war, the civil war, and the Korean war. In 1953 the new leadership in Peking launched its first five-year plan. Designed to speed up the process of industrialization, it stressed agricultural collectivization and the concentration of capital and labor in key industrializing projects. The Japanese economic connection was not considered essential in this enterprise. For one thing, foreign trade was not viewed as a major source of revenue, and it played only a minor role in economic planning. The same was true of foreign borrowing. To the extent that China turned to external sources for its industrialization projects, it was primarily the Soviet Union that provided technology, personnel, machinery, and capital throughout the 1950s. It seems that some 430 million dollars were provided to China by the Soviet Union—quite close to the amount paid Japan by the United States through its special procurement orders during the Korean war—but about 30 percent of this had to be expended in connection with the war effort, another contrast to the Japanese case. In such a situation economic ties between China and Japan were not central to the picture.

It is all the more remarkable, therefore, that even in those days there were signs of what would develop into the so-called separation of politics and economics in Chinese-Japanese relations. In our context this separation denotes a gap between the power and economic aspects of the bilateral relationship. Despite their respective alliance systems and despite the absence of a formal diplomatic relationship, Chinese and Japanese exchanged trade missions and sought to find ways to expand trade. In 1955 China sent its first trade mission to Japan, consisting of thirty-eight delegates. They were particularly eager to persuade the Japanese to sell more to China. Heretofore, reversing the trend in the immediate postwar years, the trade had been in China's favor, but that country wanted a more balanced relationship, perhaps because Japan produced much that China needed which could not be supplied by the Soviet Union or other countries willing to trade with Peking. The trade negotiations were partially successful in this regard in that the resulting agreement stipulated the stationing of a trade mission in each country as well as the opening of trade fairs in both. Though limited in scope, even this degree of commercial ties was in sharp contrast to the virtual cessation of trade with the People's Republic of China on the part of the United States and most of its Asian allies. It also indicated that the Cold War framework was not entirely successful in overcoming a determined eagerness on the part of the Japanese to expand export trade in all directions, China included, in order to speed the process of economic growth. The Chinese, for their part, were anxious to take advantage of this interest in order to obtain much needed goods, especially industrial machinery as it planned for further industrialization.

In connection with its second five-year plan, which was designed as a program for the development of heavy industry during 1958–1962, the Chinese negotiated for a sale of 400 million dollars worth of machinery and equipment from Japan and for an agreement that provided for a long-term supply of iron and steel from that country. These promising beginnings were followed by a few years of drastic cutbacks in Chinese-Japanese economic relations in the late 1950s and the early 1960s. Nevertheless, the overall trend in these relations was unmistakable.

The deepening economic ties ensured that the cultural ties that had been maintained despite the postwar confusion in Japan and China would be sustained. Here again it must be recognized that China's main cultural connection at the time was with the Soviet Union, and Japan's with the United States. Between 1950 and 1956 some 7,500 Chinese students studied in Russia, and about 3,000 Japanese students in the United States; there was no exchange between China and Japan. Still, instances of cultural contact abounded. For example, the Red Cross organizations of both countries arranged for the repatriation of Japanese civilians, numbering around 30,000, from China, and in 1954 a ten-person Chinese Red Cross mission visited Japan, the first such visit by an official Chinese organization. The visitors and the Japanese hosts emphasized that the affair symbolized the determination of the two peoples to maintain cordial relations even when their governments did not deal with each other officially. As Li Te-ch'üan, head of the Chinese delegation, remarked, the two peoples were intent upon strengthening their economic and cultural ties. As if to prove this, in the mid-1950s not only economic missions but academic and cultural delegations were exchanged.

One high point came when members of the Chinese Academy of Science visited Japan in late 1955. The delegation was headed by Kuo Mo-jo who, as already noted, had kept in touch with Japanese intellectuals after the war. He had spent twenty years in Japan before the war, so this was a return visit to his second home. Kuo conversed in Japanese with his hosts, who included literary figures as well as politicians. The Japanese expressed their admiration for China's nation-building under the Communist leadership, and Kuo insisted that the revolution was similar in spirit to the Meiji Restoration. There was a great deal of goodwill on both sides, and Kuo's visit was followed by exhanges of doctors, scientists, agricultural experts, labor union representatives, and many others. A Kabuki troupe performed in Chinese cities, a Peking opera company in Japanese cities. The establishment at this time of the Chinese People's Association for External Cultural Exchange and, in Japan, of the Association for Japanese-Chinese Cultural Exchange provided an institutional framework for maintaining these activities on a long-term basis.[10]

It cannot be said that these instances of cultural contact had a direct impact on the two countries' official relations. At the level of power politics and security considerations, they remained within their respective alliance systems. But the cultural ties may have helped sustain and promote the developing economic connections, thereby confirming the separation of politics and economics. It is possible that in time the economic and cultural ties might have grown to such an extent that pressures might have been generated for normalizing diplomatic relations between China and Japan. But few expected such a change in the near future, and in the meantime the gap between the power and the other aspects of Chinese-Japanese relations remained wide.

The gap might have been bridged if a strong pacifist or neutralist sentiment had developed among the Japanese people, turning them against the American security alliance and toward embracing China as a potential ally, not a hypothetical enemy in the framework of the Cold War. Pacifists and neutralists do seem to have grown in number and influence in Japan during the 1950s, particularly in the aftermath of the *Lucky Dragon* affair of 1954, in which American hydrogen-bomb tests in the Bikini atoll caused the death of a Japanese fisherman. When Japanese antinuclear activists held their first world congress against atomic and hydrogen bombs in Hiroshima in 1955, China sent a high-level delegation, consisting of representatives from commerce, industry, the arts, and even religious groups. Prime Minister Chou En-lai played upon Japan's nuclear fear and attacked the United States for its wartime atomic bombing as well as postwar tests. In time all this might have generated a groundswell of popular protest in Japan—in a sense the antisecurity treaty riots of 1960 were one dramatic instance of this—so that the American-Japanese security system might have become seriously strained.

That this did not happen may, paradoxically, be understood as a cultural phenomenon of the 1950s. Postwar Japanese society had been characterized by the eclipse of the military and the resurgence to positions of influence on the part of civilian bureaucrats, party politicians, businessmen, and intellectuals. They spelled the reassertion of economic and cultural pursuits as national priorities. However, Japanese economic and cultural affairs were much more closely linked to the United States than to China; there was a certain coherence in the power, economic, and cultural aspects of U.S.-Japanese relations. To reorient Japanese foreign policy away from the American alliance and toward closer ties to China would have required that Japan's economic and cultural elites consciously decide to call for that option, and that China make it a policy to encourage such a trend.

There was some of both in the mid-1950s. The Bandung conference of 1955, in which Chou En-lai radiated sympathy and understanding for neutralist forces, attracted much interest in Japan and might have generated a strong movement for neutralism there. The widespread sentiment in favor of reconciliation with China would have been reinforced by such a movement. Rōyama Masamichi, a respected scholar of political affairs, was expressing a typical opinion of this sort when he wrote in 1957 that, although Japan's aggressive behavior in China after 1931 had created an "unnatural situation" in Chinese-Japanese relations, the two peoples had a long record of friendly association that should be renewed now that the Chinese appeared to be extending their hands to the Japanese. It was a moral imperative for both peoples to effect reconciliation.[11]

Such reconciliation was doomed to be postponed for more than ten years. To inquire why is to turn to the themes of the next subperiod in the postwar history of Chinese-Japanese relations, covering the period from the late 1950s to the late 1960s. These years saw the climax of the Cold

War—or it might be better to say a transition from one Cold War to another. The United States and the Soviet Union were now more or less evenly matched in military terms. Whereas in 1963 the Soviet Union was estimated to be spending about 25 billion dollars on defense, half as much as the United States, ten years later the figures for both countries were closer: 54 billion dollars for the U.S.S.R. and 52 for the U.S. This catching up on the Soviet side was dramatically demonstrated by the 1957 Sputnik launching and the Cuban missile installation of 1962, both designed to achieve overall nuclear equilibrium with the United States. The Cold War in the sense of a nuclear arms race thus intensified and even threatened to lead to a third World War. At the same time, for the first time since the Second World War the two superpowers began negotiating for some restraint on the arms race and succeeded, in 1963, in signing a partial nuclear test-ban treaty. This was followed in 1968 by the conclusion of a nuclear nonproliferation treaty. There were frequent meetings of the American and Soviet leaders to confirm these agreements and to ensure that a nuclear war would not come about through some misunderstanding or the magnifying of local conflicts. These years can be viewed as the time when the power relationship between the two nuclear superpowers became somewhat stabilized. Whether this was called a balance of terror (the so-called MAD, mutually assured destruction) or a new structure of peace (as Henry Kissinger would say in the early 1970s), it appeared possible that the two hegemonic powers would honor the strategic status quo in the world. This was confirmed when neither the American bombing of North Vietnam nor the Soviet invasion of Czechoslovakia was allowed to stand in the way of the U.S.-Soviet nuclear understanding.

Paradoxically, such stabilization in superpower relations complicated rather than improved Chinese-Japanese relations, at least at the power level. It might have been expected that, as the United States and the Soviet Union redefined their relationship, Japan and China, tied to the superpowers, would do likewise. In reality, the Asian neighbors became if anything more distanced from each other than at any time since 1949. This was because the Chinese leadership chose not to support the U.S.-Soviet rapprochement, thereby alienating China from both superpowers, whereas the Japanese welcomed the rapprochement and fitted themselves into the new scheme. While they solidified their security ties to the United States, they also maintained a "low posture" on defense, thus managing not to antagonize the Soviet Union. The result was Chinese-Japanese estrangement in regional security issues. This estrangement would have become even more serious if it had been accompanied by acute economic and cultural tensions. Such was not the case. Economically at least, the ties between the two countries became stronger, while in the cultural sphere the picture was enormously complicated not only because of China's Cultural Revolution but also because Japanese opinion became fascinated by the global revolutionary movements, a phenomenon aptly called "counterculture" in the United States. The 1960s were a decade of profound cultural change, and China and America were among the most pronounced examples. Japan did not remain unaffected, and its leaders and public opinion were forced to redefine the nature of their foreign affairs.

All these developments made for often contradictory trends in Chinese-Japanese relations. At the power level this period was notable because of China's emergence as the world's third military power insofar as defense spending was concerned. Although these figures cannot be precise or definitive, statistically it may be noted that whereas Britain and France had spent as much, or more than, China prior to the late 1950s, now the latter surpassed them. China was the only country outside the two nuclear giants to spend more than 10 billion dollars on defense, a figure that was less than a fourth of the American or the Soviet military budget but more than the British and French defense spending combined.

If the Soviet-Chinese alliance had remained solid, the global military balance might have tipped in favor of that alliance against the Western bloc. But from the late 1950s onward, Moscow and Peking steadily drifted apart. Even as the United States and the Soviet Union stabilized their power-level relations on the basis of a rough nuclear balance, China refused to be incorporated into the new arrangement, instead developing its own nuclear armament and mobilizing the masses for what was called a people's war against imperialism and, eventually, even against Soviet "revisionism." This was a term that connoted a country (and its leadership) that had abandoned the commitment to Marxism-Leninism, the most cardinal principle of which should have been constant struggle against imperialism. Soon the Chinese would be calling both the United States and Russia "hegemonic powers," against which the rest of the world, particularly the Third World countries, must fight. In 1964 Mao Tse-tung ordered war preparations against imperialism and revisionism, and China was divided into three areas: the coastal cities; the hinterland into which their factories and equipment were to be removed; and zones in between. Between 1965 and 1968 some 320,000 military personnel were sent to Vietnam in order to demonstrate China's support for what was seen as a global anti-imperialistic struggle, which, after the Soviet invasion of Czechoslovakia in 1968, was redefined to include the conflict with the "social imperialists"—namely, the Soviets. The following year saw skirmishes between Chinese and Soviet forces along the Siberian border.

Japan's behavior was in sharp contrast to China's. Even as the latter alienated itself from the major powers of the world, Japan took steps to strengthen its ties to the United States. As a result, tensions between the two Asian nations grew. The first clear sign of this came in the late 1950s, when Prime Minister Kishi Nobusuke traveled to Taiwan and Southeast Asia, the first such undertaking by a Japanese leader after the war. For Kishi, a former "class A" war criminal, visiting these neighboring countries was a way of expressing his eagerness to bring the war to a formal end. He initiated discussions for reparations payments to the countries Japanese troops had occupied and sought to establish a new relationship with them within the framework of the Asian security system. But the fact that he did little to improve relations with Peking was a clear signal that Japan was determined to remain allied to the United States in security matters. This appeared to be confirmed when Tokyo and Washington signed a revised security pact in 1960, an arrangement that would perpetuate the military alliance within the framework of the Cold War.

Peking's response was quick and unambiguous. The Chinese government denounced Kishi's Asian trips and the 1960 U.S.-Japanese treaty as unmistakable signs of a revival of militarism in Japan. There was some genuine fear in Japan at that time that Chinese-Japanese relations were being damaged beyond repair. Yet, despite such a crisis atmosphere, there was no overt military confrontation. Japan did not become directly involved in the U.S.-Chinese conflict in

Vietnam or elsewhere. Nor did it play a role as America's security partner; it did not assist the United States in the war in Vietnam or take sides when war broke out between China and India in 1962, a war in which the United States explicitly sided with India. Even more important, Japan did not strengthen its defenses as befitting an ally of the United States. While its GNP tripled during the ten years following the end of the Korean war, as did government outlays, defense expenditures did not even double and their share of the GNP dropped to about 1.5 percent. The trend continued under Prime Minister Ikeda Hayato's "income-doubling" strategy. This policy, begun in 1964, resulted in yet another tripling of national income in the next five years, whereas defense spending barely doubled. While China continued to build up its military power, Japan did not keep pace. The result was an asymmetrical pattern of Chinese-Japanese relations at this level.

Such a pattern in itself might have proven destabilizing. After all, a China growing stronger militarily, but alienated from the superpowers, and a Japan still holding to its strategy of minimal arms build-ups, but tied to American military power, were not a likely pair for a stable bilateral relationship. What prevented a more serious confrontation was the two countries' economic connection, which, after a brief hiatus in 1958–1962, grew closer, as if to belie the significance of the military factor in Chinese-Japanese relations.

For a time it seemed as though the bilateral trade might reflect the power-level tensions, reversing the earlier trends toward an expanding commercial contact. Following the Nagasaki flag incident of 1958—when a Chinese flag was hauled down by a Japanese at a trade fair—which led the Peking authorities to terminate all trade agreements, Japanese export to China suffered a precipitous decline. It plummeted from over 25 billion yen in 1957 down to less than a billion yen in 1960, and it was three years before it recovered the level of the mid-1950s. Because Japan's overall export trade doubled between 1957 and 1963, this indicated the diminishing importance of the China market for Japanese commerce overall. Put another way, the separation of politics from economics, or the gap between the power and economic aspects of Chinese-Japanese relations, seemed to be narrowing.

But then, quite abruptly, this brief reversal was followed by unprecedented expansion in the bilateral trade. It is important to keep in mind that in military and diplomatic terms nothing really changed in Chinese-Japanese relations. Peking continued to assail Japanese imperialism as part of "the counterrevolutionary global strategy of American imperialism"; and Tokyo, for its part, steadfastly refused to alter its strategic ties to the United States. Despite this, trade between the two countries picked up momentum; the total figures increased from about 136 million dollars in 1963 to 470 million in 1965, 560 million in 1967, and 630 million in 1969. Suddenly Japan found itself the top trade partner of China, accounting for 15 to 20 percent of the latter's trade annually. While China's share in Japanese trade never exceeded 3 percent, it is significant that in the second half of the 1960s Japan for the first time in postwar history recorded net trade surpluses and that China and the United States were the two principal countries that began to buy more from than sell to Japan.

How can we account for this phenomenon? Obviously the two countries were determined not to allow their power-level antagonism to stand in the way of economic interests. The so-called LT arrangements, worked out by Liao Cheng-Chih and Takasaki Tatsunosuke in 1962, specified that Japan would sell China fertilizer, steel, and agricultural machinery and implements, while buying from it coal, soybeans, and other commodities. Even more important, under the arrangements each country established a trade office in the other, indicating a commitment for a long-term association.

For the Chinese leaders these steps, whatever their strategic implications, were justifiable in view of the abrupt halt in Soviet economic and technical assistance. After 1960, when Soviet engineers and advisers were withdrawn and hundreds of cooperative projects scrapped, it must have seemed desirable to turn elsewhere to compensate for this turn of events. Whereas up to that point trade with other Communist countries accounted for 60 to 70 percent of overall Chinese trade, in the 1960s this share steadily declined, until in 1969 it fell to a mere 20 percent, the other 80 percent being trade with non-Communist countries. Even then Chinese trade amounted to only 3,860 million dollars, about one-tenth of Japan's. China was still going through the phase of "self-help," to reduce dependence on foreign nations and achieve a measure of economic independence through the establishment of a national economy. These themes would be emphasized with particular vigor during the Cultural Revolution, begun in 1966. The fact remains that trade with Japan increased in importance throughout these years. Economic relations had a momentum of their own, not totally controlled by military or ideological considerations. How such a gap could be explained to themselves or to the people was a problem the Chinese leaders would have to grapple with eventually. For the time being, the gap between the power and economic dimensions of Chinese-Japanese relations was a reminder that not even a state with a doctrinaire foreign policy was free from the often contradictory crosscurrents among the various aspects of its international affairs.

In Japan the gap between the power and economic factors was different. This was a period of self-conscious economic expansion, and the eagerness for trade with China, despite the constraints dictated by security considerations, indicated how much economics had come to dominate national affairs. As Prime Minister Ikeda noted, economics rather than politics was binding the nations of Europe closer together, and Japan as well as other countries of Asia could do likewise. Characteristically, Ikeda defined the "free world" in economic terms, asserting that North America, Europe, and Japan were its "three pillars."[12] He was undoubtedly speaking for Japan's civilian leadership, businessmen, and the majority of the emerging middle class. The primacy of economics in Japanese policy can only be understood as a consensus produced by these groups. This consensus, however, contained a serious gap between military policy, where Japan would continue to depend on America's "nuclear umbrella" for protection, and trade policy, which would push for expansion of Japanese exports in all directions. The gap was there, but it did not yet present a serious problem since on the whole the world at that time tolerated such an orientation in Japanese foreign policy. Certainly the United States did not oppose Japanese trade with China, while Peking saw little contradiction between the bilateral trade and the power-level antagonism. All these factors served to promote Japanese export to China. It is interesting that those Japanese who were then engaged in the sale of chemical fertilizers and steel to China were so solicitous of the trade that they were willing to offer favorable terms, including extension of credits and even the building of industrial plants. These would become key themes in Chinese-Japanese economic relations in the subsequent decades.

Culturally the picture was more complicated, particularly in the second half of the 1960s which saw a drastic reduction of cultural contact between the two peoples because of the Cultural Revolution. Until then, their "friendly exchanges," as the phenomenon was called, continued to grow. One climax came in 1965, when the first gathering of Chinese and Japanese youths was held in fifteen Chinese cities. More than 500 Japanese were sent to China; while there, they met Chairman Mao, who exhorted the young people of the two nations to work together against their common enemy, the American imperialists.[13] Another 3,300 Japanese visited China in the same year, while Japan received 400 Chinese visitors. Several newspaper correspondents resided in each other's capital, as stipulated in a 1964 trade agreement.

But then Chinese cultural and political life was thrown into turmoil, and very few people-to-people exchanges were undertaken between the two countries during the Cultural Revolution. The origins or the progress of the Cultural Revolution had little or nothing to do with Japan directly, but it had the effect of temporarily cutting off noneconomic ties between the two peoples. Japanese journalists and businessmen were expelled from China, accused of spying. Japanese of long residence in China, including the "war orphans" who had been cared for by Chinese foster parents, were often persecuted. Liao Ch'eng-chih and other officials identified with the promotion of Chinese-Japanese communication came under attack. And, as the Japanese Communist party denounced the Cultural Revolution, many organizations in Japan under its influence lost their standing in China.

An interesting question in this connection is the extent to which the Cultural Revolution affected Japanese cultural affairs. A substantial industry in Japan has developed, devoted to unearthing statements made by influential leaders in the late 1960s and the early 1970s in praise of the Cultural Revolution; its principal objective is to embarrass and discredit them as opinionmakers. Undoubtedly large segments of the Japanese mass media as well as the scholarly community fell under the spell of the revolutionary developments in the neighboring country and sought to transmit some of the same spirit to Japan. The timing seemed just right, as Japanese opinion was becoming more and more critical of the American war in Vietnam as well as of the Tokyo government's staunch adherence to the security treaty, renewed in 1970. The revolutionary fervor—found not only in China but also in France, Germany, the United States, and elsewhere—spread to Japan, and between 1969 and 1972 there were as many instances of student radicalism and violence there as in other parts of the world.

Such a situation might have generated forces for Japan's own cultural revolution, alienating Japanese from Americans and strengthening ties of empathy between Chinese and Japanese. That this did not happen can be attributed to a number of factors. A key one was greater Japanese admiration for, and identification with, the social and cultural movements in the United States, which seemed to confirm that country's pluralism and commitment to reform, in contrast to the much greater destructiveness and dogmatism of the Chinese movement. It also helped that throughout the 1960s academic and cultural exchanges between the United States and Japan continued to grow, so that the young intellectual and journalistic leaders who emerged as experts on America could speak from personal experience, whereas much that was said or written about China had to be based on indirect knowledge.

Nevertheless, worldwide countercultural movements, as well as China's Cultural Revolution, in addition to the U.S.-Soviet rapprochement in nuclear matters, might have generated forces within Japan for a drastic reorientation of its foreign affairs. There were in fact voices calling for a new definition of Japanese diplomacy, now that the nation had fully recovered from the war and world conditions were fast changing. During the 1960s many in Japan recognized the need to pay closer attention to Asia than had been the case after the war. Even a leader as committed to the American alliance as Prime Minister Satō Eisaku remarked, in 1969, that as Asia's preeminent industrial nation, Japan had an obligation to help create a condition in the region where countries of different ethnic, religious, and cultural traditions would prosper together in peace.[14] The language here was reminiscent of the pan-Asianist rhetoric of the 1930s. The difference was that Satō spoke of the need for Japan to cooperate with the United States in carrying out its Asian tasks and of "nonmilitary," that is, "economic and technical," sorts of assistance that the nation should offer its neighbors.

This was as developed a vision as could be found in the 1960s, one inherently capable of building bridges between China and the United States. Such a vision seems to have had the support of the Japanese people, who saw no contradiction between the American security treaty and the maintenance of economic and cultural ties to China. But because the vision was not meant to offer a radical alternative to the U.S.-Japanese alliance, the search for a comprehensive definition of Japanese foreign policy would continue.

In the absence of a cultural initiative, the primacy of economics in Japanese foreign affairs remained. This preoccupation with economic affairs, in a world in which most nations still defined foreign relations in power terms, may have prepared the country well to cope with the global changes of the 1970s and the 1980s, when the critical importance of economic issues in international affairs came to be recognized and even to overshadow the military-security aspect. The global economy entered a period of profound transformation, in the process creating instability, dislocation, and disequilibrium. As a result, one key story of international affairs in the last twenty years has been that of adjusting to this economic transformation, to shift from a Cold-War type of world system defined by military power to something different, although what this something is has become clear only in rough outline.

During the 1970s economic affairs began to have a momentum of their own, often quite unrelated to the structure of power relations. Henry Kissinger described the situation graphically as early as 1971, when he said that the United States was engaged in an "economic war" against its European allies. Two years later he accused these same allies of continuing to rely on the United States for their security but engaging in "confrontation and even hostility" toward America on the economic front. What was happening of course was the rise of the western European countries to economic power, which, increasingly in cooperation with one another, was presenting a serious challenge to the United States just when it was beginning to be plagued by inflation, balance-of-payments deficits, and a constant drain of the gold reserve. The crisis would culminate in the scrapping of the Bretton Woods system of world monetary transactions and an end to the postwar structure of trade based on the principle of dollar convertibility to gold. As if this were not enough, the oil crisis of 1973, followed by another six years later, brought about double-digit inflations in most advanced capitalist countries, while further intensifying their trade rivalry in order to pay for the tripled and quadrupled prices of imported petroleum. In the meantime, Third World countries began to stress, not so much their neutrality in the Cold War, as the need for what they called "a new economic order" that would incorporate the economic rights of developing nations and arrest the tendency toward widening gaps between rich and poor countries.

The confusion and instability these new developments produced were in sharp contrast to the geopolitical aspect of international relations. This aspect was now characterized not only by the continued detente between the United States and the Soviet Union but also by a reversal in U.S.-Chinese relations. Starting with Henry Kissinger's trip to Peking in 1971, China became steadily incorporated into the global balance-of-power system. The U.S.-Chinese rapprochement facilitated the ending of the Vietnam war and the American withdrawal from Southeast Asia. The power-level structure of international affairs was now characterized as multipolar or polycentric. Although the domination of the United States and the Soviet Union in nuclear terms did not change, China was now a full-fledged great power, and among the three some sort of military balance was postulated. Because all three were ultimately committed to maintaining the status quo, the relationship between what had hitherto been two camps also grew more stable.

These developments provided favorable conditions for a redefinition of Chinese-Japanese relations. Actually it may be more accurate to say that the primacy of economics in the bilateral relationship needed no redefinition, but that it was now backed up by a degree of understanding on security issues, so that the gap between the power and economic dimensions of Chinese-Japanese relations narrowed considerably. To the extent that the world of the 1970s was characterized by some sort of big-power balance and by global economic disorder, it may be said that the Chinese and Japanese, because of the nature of their association during the 1950s and the 1960s, were in a good position to respond to these changes. They would normalize their diplomatic relations and at the same time undertake further extension of their economic links.

To be sure, the normalization itself was not a product of any initiative on either side or a result of the two countries' deepening commercial ties; it was purely a byproduct of changes in the American geopolitical strategy. Japan, having failed to anticipate the U.S.-Chinese rapprochement, had to adjust literally overnight to the new development and the creation of a situation in Asia in which Washington would recognize Peking's role in regional stabilization and reduce U.S. military power in the area.

Japan's response was to follow the American lead and establish normal diplomatic relations with Peking. This came about in September 1972 and entailed several aspects. First, although "normalization" did not amount to a peace treaty, which would not be signed until 1978, Japan now formally expressed regret over the suffering the war had caused the Chinese people. Second, the Japanese government made it clear that the peace treaty it had signed with the Nationalist regime in Taipei in 1952 would lapse. Third, the Chinese government agreed to give up its claims to war reparations from Japan. This was an expression of Chinese magnanimity, especially in view of the fact that the Chinese had suffered more than any other people from the Japanese war and that writer after writer in China had asserted that reparations must be paid to help the country recover economically. The Peking authorities undoubtedly reasoned that by being generous on this score, the Japanese could be induced to offer various types of economic assistance and to cooperate with China in promoting regional stability.

This desire for stability was a departure from the earlier emphasis on wars of national liberation or on the people's anti-imperialistic struggle. It revealed Peking's concern over the deteriorating relationship with Moscow and its eagerness for an effective counterweight to the Soviet Union through ties to the United States and Japan. Both the U.S.-Chinese communiqué of February 1972 and the Chinese-Japanese communiqué seven months later contained a passage, identical in language, opposing hegemony: "neither power should seek hegemony in the Asia-Pacific region, and each is opposed to the efforts by any other country or group of countries to seek such hegemony." Because the reference to "hegemony" obviously referred to the Soviet Union, the Japanese hesitated to accept the phraseology. But in the end they decided to do so and joined China in what amounted to a new power system in Asia. In that system the Chinese not only no longer objected to the U.S.-Japanese security treaty, and even expressed support for it because of its potential usefulness against Soviet power. Thus China was becoming a de-facto strategic partner of the United States and Japan, a development that did not necessarily fit into the overall framework of the U.S.-Soviet detente but which nevertheless could complement it and bring about a more stable international order.

All this was welcome news to the Japanese, but they responded by persisting in a low defensive posture rather than by augmenting their relative military power in the wake of the retrenchment of American power in the region. Tokyo let it be known that the nation would not spend more than 1 percent of its GNP on defense. In fact, the ratio of defense expenditures to Japan's GNP ranged from 0.8 to 0.9 percent during the 1970s. Because the United States too reduced military spending, devoting 8.2 percent of its GNP on arms in 1970 (the postwar high) but only 4.8 percent in 1978, while the Soviet Union continued to increase its military budgets, the Chinese fear of the Soviet menace may in part have been justified. But if China wanted Japan to do something about it, that country did not oblige. Its 1976 "guidelines for defense planning," which remained the cardinal document for Japanese defense policy until the early 1990s, declared that the nation would persist in a purely defensive strategy, augmenting its arms only to the degree necessary to deter aggression. Otherwise, Japan would continue to count on American protection. Overall what was remarkable about the 1970s was that in terms of military power Chinese-Japanese relations gained a level of stability not seen since the war.

Such a situation made it easier for the two countries to solidify economic ties. This was an achievement in itself, inasmuch as the decade was characterized by growing tensions and uncertainty in international economic affairs. Japanese economic relations with the United States reflected this. It may have been symbolic that when President Richard Nixon met Prime Minister Tanaka Kakuei in Hawaii in August 1972, shortly before Tanaka's trip to China, they dealt both with the security question, in which the two leaders pledged continued cooperation under the alliance system, and the economic issue, where Japan's export surpluses were giving rise to serious friction. From this time on trade disputes would loom larger and larger in relations between the two allies. Economic affairs were increasingly overshadowing military-strategic affairs among the Western allies, and U.S.-Japanese relations were no exception.

Under the circumstances the growth of Chinese-Japanese economic relations was an area of certainty. The Japanese moved swiftly to take advantage of the rapprochement with the People's Republic in order to expand trade and investment opportunities there. They were well prepared to do so, having paid close attention to economic ties with China for many years. It must have been relatively easy for Japanese businessmen to build on past achievements and bring more goods to China now that official relations between the two countries had been established. The bilateral trade doubled almost overnight between 1972 and 1973 and nearly tripled in the next five years. Japan retained its position as China's leading trading partner. China's share of Japan's overall trade remained low, less than 3 percent, but there were significant new developments. For example, Japan began buying petroleum from China for the first time, just in time for the oil shocks, and extended long-term credits to China for plant construction. Within a year after the normalization, twelve projects, amounting to 660 million dollars, had been contracted for, including chemical and fire-power plants, far more than the 200 million dollars that had been invested for similar purposes during the 1960s.

Clearly, China was reorienting its economic policy, away from self-help and toward obtaining foreign capital and technology to speed up its modernization programs. Japan, though not the only provider, was one of the first to take advantage of the change. To be sure, not everything worked out as expected. Japanese businessmen were taken aback whenever Chinese leaders reversed or modified their plans in disregard of contracts, as happened in 1981 when they announced that they were suspending the construction of iron, petroleum, and chemical plants that had been in the works with Japanese capital and technology. The convulsion in Chinese-Japanese economic relations was not exceptional at a time when international economic relations on the whole had become unhinged. It probably reflected the unmanageability, as well as the promise, of increasing economic interactions throughout the world. The fact remains that for Japan, whose share in world trade increased from 6 to 8 percent during the 1970s, China provided an important market whose continued growth could be counted upon.

Was there a corresponding increase in cultural ties between the two countries? The picture is far less clear than the one of the power and economic dimensions. For China the decade of the 1970s was one of internal reckoning, with each succeeding leadership trying to reestablish a sense of order. In the process they were attempting to rehabilitate many people—apparently as many as three million—from the indignities they had suffered during the Cultural Revolution. Teng Hsiao-p'ing, once in power, began calling for "the liberalization of thought," freeing Chinese minds from dogmatic subservience to Maoism. Henceforth the stress was to be on technical expertise and skills to promote the country's modernization. This would necessitate reform of the educational system in order to train a large number of scientists and engineers. It was not yet clear, however, how far the modernization project would be pushed, and especially to what extent "the liberalization of thought" could be encouraged without giving rise to what would soon be called "spiritual pollution" as a result of the inevitable contact with the outside world. On the whole it may be said that, just as Japan had pursued a policy of separating politics from economics, the post-Cultural-Revolution Chinese leadership sought to separate culture from economics so that economic transformation—in 1979 Teng spoke of quadrupling China's per-capita income by the end of the century—could take place without embracing bourgeois ideas or attitudes.

Such a stance perhaps was not as problematic as it would become in the late 1980s, in part because the world of the 1970s was so preoccupied with economic affairs that China's modernization programs won the attention and admiration of other countries without much criticism of its cultural exclusiveness. The lack of a more open cultural policy was reflected in the initial caution shown by Chinese leaders in resuming cultural ties with capitalist countries. A Japanese journalist who had spent his lifetime promoting people-to-people exchanges between the two countries lamented in 1981 that the Chinese leaders appeared to have lost their enthusiasm for such activities, being much more intent on mingling with high foreign officials and businessmen who could help in the modernization effort.[15]

In Japan this situation induced an attitude of caution with respect to noneconomic areas of contact with China. While the diplomatic landmarks of 1972 and 1978 had the over-whelming support of the Japanese people, rapidly changing events inside China created bewilderment. Those who had ardently worshiped the Cultural Revolution no longer could keep up with the shifts and turns in Chinese official ideology. They may have yielded their position as China experts, as makers of favorable images about the neighboring country, to those who were more pragmatic and inclined to view China as essentially no different from any other nation in pursuit of self-interest. If anything, the Chinese invasion of Vietnam in 1979 suggested that people's democracies could be just as belligerent and imperialistic as capitalist nations. Japanese socialists and radicals were dismayed when the Chinese began defending, rather than denouncing, the

U.S.-Japanese security treaty, and even arguing for Japan's increased armament. If China was behaving like any other country in terms of geopolitical considerations and economic objectives, then Japan might compare favorably with it. Because Japan was spending proportionately less on armament and doing better economically, a sense of self-satisfaction, even superiority, over China may have been generated for the first time since the war.

Given this background, it is interesting to recall that the Japanese government throughout the 1970s had laid particular stress on cultural exchange as a foreign policy agenda. Having attained much in the economic sphere and having eschewed the road to military great-power status, Japan was about to define its foreign policy in the cultural realm. In the words of Prime Minister Ōhira, the nation would develop a "comprehensive security system" including national defense, diplomacy, economic resources, and cultural creativity. Once again Japanese leaders spoke of culture, a throwback to the 1930s and the immediate postwar years. But perhaps it was symbolic that Ōhira went to Peking to stress the cultural basis of foreign relations, asserting that the Chinese and the Japanese shared a two-thousand-year history of cultural exchange and that a correct relationship between the two countries must be built on trust, which in turn hinged on "heart-to-heart" bonds between the peoples.[16] As if to respond to such exhortations, the number of students and tourists increased steadily after the 1978 peace treaty. In 1980 alone, 1,500 Chinese students went to Japan, while nearly 6,000 Japanese students, scholars, and tourists visited China.

Whether such phenomena really built lasting cultural ties between China and Japan remained to be seen; indeed the history of the 1980s was to show how much more needed to be accomplished. Even though the decade is too recent to enable us to have a balanced perspective, it is possible that it is in the cultural sphere that Chinese-Japanese relations have had notable successes as well as frustrations, and that this rise in the importance of cultural issues reflects a key trend in the contemporary world.

The contemporary world seems to be characterized by global cultural interdependence. Thanks to revolutionary developments in communications technology, events in all parts of the world are transmitted to, and come to be known by, people elsewhere. What a segment of them experiences is a matter of concern to the rest. There is a widely shared concern with human rights, the plight of refugees, the protection of the natural environment, and drug abuse. Such cultural interdependence has been fostered by crosscultural economic transactions—not just trade and investment, but the establishment of multinational corporations and the transfer of capital, labor, and technology where opportunities beckon. Cultural interdependence signals the erosion of the state's authority in many parts of the world. No longer can the state be the commanding presence dictating all aspects of people's lives. There are communities and individuals—the "civic society"—whose boundaries do not coincide with those of the nation-states. Territorial states continue to be the key organizing principle in human affairs, and nationalism, in the sense of patriotic support for one's country or the pursuit of self-centered objectives defined as national interests, remains strong, but the nation-state is no longer the only or even the most important ingredient in the international community. Regional groupings, nongovernmental organizations, and cross-national arrangements are increasing in importance.

Recent and contemporary Chinese-Japanese relations reflect this cultural phenomenon. Student exchange programs have continued to flourish between the two countries, despite occasional interruptions such as that caused by the Tiananmen incident of June 1989. The steady stream of Chinese students coming to Japan reached 18,000 by 1990, by far the largest contingent (over 40 percent) of foreign students in the country. In addition, in the last several years thousands have gone to Japan as "language students," those with private funds ostensibly to study the language but in reality seeking employment in menial jobs. The uncertainty of their status, and the unscrupulousness of the middlemen, in both China and Japan, to profit as brokers, have plagued the exchange program. But this is part of a larger issue, that of opening Japan up to a diverse group of foreign visitors and residents. The issue transcends student exchanges and confronts the country with the task of defining its position in the world at a time when waves of refugees, legal and illegal immigrants, and other migrants are engulfing the globe. This is a key theme in international affairs today, one of the cultural themes of our time.

At the scholarly level, the recent years have been notable because of active collaboration between Chinese and Japanese academics, journalists, and others in many fields. Particularly significant have been joint projects examining the modern history of Chinese-Japanese relations. Historians from both countries have organized symposia on the war, undertaken research into the "rape of Nanking," and translated each other's works. A related development has been the often strident criticism of Japanese history textbooks by Chinese officials, scholars, and students. Starting in 1982, the complacent view of Japanese military power that had prevailed in China during the 1970s has been replaced by strong denunciations of Japan's militarism, past and present. While Chinese attacks on Japanese textbooks and reminders of Japan's war guilt are undoubtedly derived, at least in part, from political considerations and tactical calculations to obtain economic and other concessions, we must note the significance of this phenomenon as yet another milestone in bilateral intellectual communication between the two peoples. It shows a growing awareness that history, especially the modern history of Chinese-Japanese relations, should be scrutinized by both sides in a common search for understanding.

Nor have the Japanese been passive receptacles of Chinese criticism. They have become keenly aware of the possibility of offering help to China in such areas as pollution control, city planning, and industrial diseases. Because Japan has had to cope with all the problems of a rapidly industrializing society, its experiences in dealing with the environmental and medical problems that accompany industrialization seem to interest Chinese officials and specialists. This is part of ongoing global developments, where it is recognized that these matters cut across national boundaries and can be solved only through transnational cooperation. Chinese-Japanese cooperation in this regard will be a good test of whether humanity is really ready to undertake transnational projects.

The same is true of human rights, in many ways the critical issue confronting humanity today. The groundswell of the democratization movement in China in recent years can be understood as an aspect of the universal aspiration for freedom and justice. Although the aspiration always may have existed, it has become a major force in international affairs only recently, precisely because the world today is defined as much by these intellectual, ideological, and cultural forces as by strategic calculations or economic interests. Unless geopolitical factors once again gain predominance in world affairs—and there is no assurance they will not—the current importance of the cultural dimension cannot help but be reinforced in the years ahead.

Chinese-Japanese relations will also be increasingly characterized by cultural issues. That is why Japan's caution regarding the suppression of freedom in China in 1989 was anachronistic. If Tokyo's leaders felt that strategic and economic considerations must weigh more heavily than human rights and democracy, they were hopelessly behind the times, as were those Chinese leaders who thought economic modernization could continue without cultural change and asserted that national rights must take precedence over human rights. (Of course Japanese and Chinese leaders may have thought that in the wake of the Cold War, economics would assume greater and greater significance. In such circumstances, they might have envisioned building some sort of a counterpart to the European Economic Community, a project in which the participation of both countries would be crucial. Human rights and other considerations, they may have believed, could be subordinated to the dictates of economic necessities. Such thinking is precisely the problem, for the primacy of economics is proving as fleeting a phenomenon as the earlier primacy of power as the principal definer of international and national affairs.)

This is not the early twentieth century, when power was the basic determinant of national and international affairs. Nor is today's world the same as that of the 1920s, when economics provided the key setting. The increasing importance of cultural factors in international affairs in the recent years is reminiscent of the 1930s, but if we are fortunate, the cultural chauvinism and self-righteousness that gave cultural sanctions to atrocities and mass murders will not be repeated. Today's cultural agenda should be oriented toward global concerns and cross-national cooperation. It remains to be seen whether the Chinese and the Japanese are equal to the challenge. Their future greatness will be determined less by economic power, still less by military power, than by the contribution they are willing to make to build a culturally interdependent world order.

——

Epilogue

The history of Chinese-Japanese relations since the late nineteenth century is extremely rich in detail and suggests many approaches to the study of international affairs. I have tried to show that by focusing on the power, cultural, and economic dimensions of the bilateral relations, we gain an appreciation of the multifaceted nature of the story.

The story must be seen in three contexts: domestic, binational, and global. Even if we limit ourselves to three dimensions of Chinese-Japanese relations, we must link them both to their respective domestic affairs and to the overall international system. Thus I suggested in Chapter 1 that the primacy of military power as a determining characteristic of the bilateral association reflected the emergence of military leaders in positions of influence in the two countries as well as the pivotal role played by military, strategic calculations in a world dominated by the Western powers—and power was fundamentally a military proposition.

After the First World War military power lost its central position in world affairs as well as in China and Japan. The picture was complicated, however, because nationalistic movements in China and elsewhere, seeking to establish independent and unified countries, needed to develop modern armed forces. Still, in China at least nationalism took the form of a struggle for tariff autonomy and for economic modernization. And during the 1920s the world's major powers tended to define power economically and were willing to make economic concessions to China. Such a situation reflected the influence of businessmen, industrialists, and bankers in those countries, including Japan.

When the economic definition of international affairs was thrown into disarray during the world Depression, the military regained influence in Japan, determined to entrench its power in domestic politics and on the Asian continent. The Chinese resisted Japan, not so much through the use of force initially as through cultural means: mass nationalism, student movements, educational campaigns. In time the Japanese too came to resort to the language of culture, hoping that the Chinese could be persuaded to accept the idea of Asian cultural renewal against Western civilization. The marriage of power and culture in Japan again reflected domestic developments, where totalitarianism created a national psychology eager to accept the rhetoric of pan-Asianism even as the nation went to war against its neighbor. Culture became a handmaiden of power, willing even to justify an aggressive war. The Chinese in the meantime developed an ideology of democratic national resistance, which, supported by intellectuals of all persuasions, could merge with the ideals being espoused in the Western democracies against totalitarian states. In that sense the Chinese-Japanese conflict was a microcosm of one prevailing theme of international affairs during the 1930s: the struggle among competing ideologies.

After the democratic coalition's victory, it was Japan's turn to redefine "culture" and make it the alternative to militarism. The new "culture" was promoted by civilian leaders, businessmen, and intellectuals who were convinced that the pursuit of economic objectives should replace the earlier emphasis on military power. China, in contrast, was weakened not only militarily but economically through a civil war that divided the nation ideologically. The two countries were in different camps in the postwar world system led by the United States and the Soviet Union. But that did not prevent leaders in the two countries from promoting economic, and sometimes even cultural, connections. Economics was the key feature of Chinese-Japanese relations during most of the postwar years, but this was not carried out in a vacuum. The history of the two countries' cultural interactions had been too well entrenched to be eradicated. And in time, as the Cold War abated and the power dimension of the bilateral relationship became more stable, it was the cultural dimension—student exchanges, joint inquiries into the past, cooperation in controlling pollution—that took on importance. This too was an aspect of international relations that came to be more and more characterized by cross-national and cross-cultural issues.

The future of Chinese-Japanese relations may include themes that are only dimly perceptible today. Military power may regain its importance, either because armed forces come to predominate the respective political systems or because the world reverts to the pre-1914 situation—or because of a combination of these two factors. It seems more likely, however, that economic affairs may increase in importance as China continues to industrialize and Japan remains eager to supply capital and technology. In time some sort of an Asian-Pacific economic community may emerge. But it is difficult to imagine that these developments will overshadow the growing cultural interdependence, not only between the two countries but throughout the world. The coming years are likely to see further breaching of national boundaries as refugees, job-seekers, businessmen, students, and (not the least important) tourists roam all over the world. They will develop a common concern for human rights, the right of all people to live with dignity and freedom. At the same time, people in different parts of the world will become increasingly vigilant in protecting endangered species and the natural environment.

The key question in such a world will be whether or not nations and peoples can cooperate across national boundaries, often transcending narrow definitions of national interest. Are the Chinese and the Japanese prepared to undertake the task? We can only hope they are, but in order to effect cooperation in the future, it will first be necessary to learn from the past. That is particularly true of the Japanese, who have committed serious offenses against the Chinese through wars and military expeditions. They will have to show that they can develop a new conception of culture that connotes a shared commitment to protect civilization, not, as in the 1930s, a self-righteous assault on other people's ways of life. The Chinese too can learn from the past, especially from the mistakes made by a doctrinaire leadership committed to its self-preservation. Above all, the two peoples need an open engagement in pursuit of common objectives. Having experienced such a variety of patterns of their mutual interaction, they may be counted upon to assume leadership roles in bringing the world a step closer to international cultural cooperation.

Notes

Index

Notes

Chapter I. Power

1. Joseph Nye, *Bound to Lead: The Changing Nature of American Power* (New York: Basic Books, 1990), pp. 174–91.
2. Michael Howard, *The Causes of Wars* (London: Temple Smith, 1983), p. 27; Paul Kennedy, *The Rise and Decline of the Great Powers* (New York: Random, 1988), passim.
3. Hatano Yoshihiro, *Chūgoku kindai gunbatsu no kenkyū* (Modern Chinese military factions; Tokyo, 1973), p. 70; Banno Masataka, ed., *Chūgoku o meguru kokusai seiji* (International affairs around China; Tokyo, 1968), p. 35.
4. Hatano, *Chūgoku kindai,* p. 98.
5. Matsushita Yoshio, *Nis-Shin sensō zengo* (The period of the Chinese-Japanese war; Tokyo, 1939), p. 115.
6. Hatano, *Chūgoku kindai,* p. 108.
7. Simiya Mikio, *Dai Nihon teiko no shiren* (The Japanese empire on trial; Tokyo, 1967), p. 70; Asahi Shinbun-sha, ed., *Shiryō Meiji hyakunen* (Documents on the last hundred years; Tokyo, 1966), p. 618.
8. These and other statistics are taken from Nik-Ka Jitsugyō Kyōkai, ed., *Shina kindai no seiji keizai* (The politics and economy of modern China; Tokyo, 1931).
9. Peter Duus et al., eds., *Japan's Informal Empire in China* (Princeton: Princeton University Press, 1989), p. 29.
10. See Kennedy, *Rise and Decline;* Alan Milward, *War, Economy, and Society* (Berkeley: University of California Press, 1979).
11. Duus, *Japan's Informal Empire,* pp. 58–59.
12. Satō Saburō, *Kindai Nit-Chū kōryū-shi no kenkyū* (Chinese-Japanese interactions in modern times; Tokyo, 1984), p. 13.
13. Andō Hikotarō, *Nihonjin no Chūgoku-kan* (Japanese images of China; Tokyo, 1967), p. 164.

14. Watanabe Ryūsaku, *Nihon to Chūgoku no hyakunen* (One hundred years of Japan and China; Tokyo, 1968), p. 103.
15. Itō Toramaru et al., eds., *Kindai bungaku ni okeru Chūgoku to Nihon* (China and Japan in modern literature; Tokyo, 1986), pp. 151–80.
16. Duus, *Japan's Informal Empire,* pp. 213–21.
17. John K. Fairbank, *The United States and China* (Cambridge, Mass.: Harvard University Press, 1987), p. 212.
18. Sanetō Keishū, *Nihon bunka no Shina e no eikyō* (The influence of Japanese culture on China; Tokyo, 1940), pp. 73–75.
19. Ibid., p. 83.
20. Ibid.
21. Nagai Kafū, *Kafū zenshū* (Collected works of Kafū; Tokyo, 1963), III, 566–67.

Chapter II. Culture

1. Fritz Stern, *Dreams and Delusions* (New York: Vintage, 1989), p. 54.
2. George Bernard Shaw, *Heartbreak House* (New York, 1919).
3. Banno, ed., *Chūgoku,* pp. 138–41.
4. Inoue Kiyoshi et al., eds., *Taishō-ki kyūshinteki jiyūshugi* (Radical liberalism in the Taishō era; Tokyo, 1972), p. 168.
5. Ibid., pp. 255–56.
6. Ibid., p. 176.
7. Gary R. Hess, *Vietnam and the United States* (Boston: Twayne, 1990), p. 15.
8. Makino Shinken, *Nikki* (Diary; Tokyo, 1990), pp. 718–21.
9. Inazo Nitobe, *Japan: Some Phases of Problems and Development* (New York: Macmillan, 1931), p. 300.
10. *Shina kindai,* p. 847.
11. Duus, *Japan's Informal Empire,* p. 113.
12. Andō, *Nihonjin no Chūgoku-kan,* p. 102; Satō, *Kindai Nit-Chū,* p. 57.
13. Duus, *Japan's Informal Empire,* p. 285.
14. Itō, *Kindai bungaku,* pp. 320–22; Robert Park, *Race and Culture* (Boston, 1945), p. 149.
15. Janet Flanner, *Paris Was Yesterday* (New York: Harcourt, 1972), p. 219.

16. William Shirer, *Berlin Journal* (Boston: Little, Brown, 1940), pp. 141–43.

17. Tokutomi Iichirō, *Manshū kenkoku dokuhon* (The building of Manchuria; Tokyo, 1940), p. 164.

18. Ibid., pp. 136–37.

19. Ibid., pp. 126–28; Haruyama Yukio, *Manshū no bunka* (Manchurian culture; Tokyo, 1943), pp. 334–36.

20. Itō, *Kindai bungaku,* pp. 529–50.

21. On the Hsin-min Hui, see my essay in Akira Iriye, ed., *The Chinese and the Japanese: Studies in Political and Cultural Interactions* (Princeton: Princeton University Press, 1980).

22. Furuta Hikaru et al., eds. *Kindai Nihon shakai shisō-shi* (History of modern Japanese social thought; Tokyo, 1971), II, 200.

23. Shirer, *Berlin Journal,* p. 233; Fritz Stern, *Politics of Cultural Despair* (Berkeley: University of California Press, 1961).

24. Furuta, *Kindai Nihon,* II, 207–08, 210, 296; Matsumoto Gaku, *Sekai shinchitsujo no bunkateki kensetsu* (The cultural construction of the new world order; Tokyo, 1940), p. 240.

25. Fujisawa Chikao, *Zentai shugi to kōdō* (Totalitarianism and the Imperial way; Tokyo, 1939), pp. 118, 124.

26. *Kokusai bunka* (International culture) 10 (August 1940); 1–2.

27. Tamura Tokuji, *Nihon to shin kokusaishugi* (Japan and the new internationalism; Kyoto, 1939), pp. 367–68.

28. Ts'ai to League of Nations, Mar. 2, 1932, Papers of Board of Education, ED25/25, Public Record Office.

29. Hirano Tadashi, *Chūgoku kakumei no chishikijin* (China's revolutionary intellectuals; Tokyo, 1977), pp. 31, 35.

30. Mizutani Kuniichi, *Kō-Nichi minzoku tōitsu sensen undō-shi* (History of the united front resistance to Japan; Dairen, 1939), pp. 154–55, 182, 184.

31. Ibid., pp. 189–202, 216.

32. Ibid., p. 373.

Chapter III. Economics

1. Chūgoku Kenkyūjo, ed., *Shohō* (Newsletter) 1 (March 1947): 26; *Chūkoku shiryō geppō* (Monthly digest of materials on China) 1 (November 1946): 57.

2. *Shohō,* 1: 10.

3. Chūgoku Bunka Kenkyūjo, ed., *Chūgoku shiryō* (Materials on China) 1 (November 1946): 1–3.
4. Ibid. 3 (August 1947): 1–3.
5. Ibid., 3: 32.
6. Furuta, *Kindai Nihon*, II, 293.
7. Akira Iriye, *Shin Nihon no gaikō* (Japan's diplomacy since the war; Tokyo, 1991), p. 50; Hoashi Riichirō, *Democrashii no shisō to shūkyō* (Democratic thought and religion; Tokyo, 1949), p. 1.
8. *Shohō* 9 (January 1948): 13.
9. Furukawa Mantarō, *Nit-Chū sengo kankei-shi* (History of postwar Chinese-Japanese relations; Tokyo, 1981), pp. 16–17.
10. Ibid., pp. 31–33.
11. Iriye, *Shin Nihon*, p. 102.
12. Ibid., p. 128.
13. Furukawa, *Nit-Chū*, pp. 245–46.
14. Iriye, *Shin Nihon*, pp. 175–76.
15. Furukawa, *Nit-Chū*, pp. 416–31.
16. Iriye, *Shin Nihon*, pp. 175–76.

Index